215 Delicious & Appetizing Classic Soup Recipes For Modern Kitchens

by
Lisa Turner

NMD Books
Simi Valley, CA

Copyright 2015 –by Lisa Turner

All rights reserved. No part of this book may be reproduced in any format or by any means without written permission from the publisher.

Library of Congress Cataloging-in-Publication

215 Delicious and Appetizing Classic Soup Recipes For Modern Kitchens

By Lisa Turner

ISBN: 978-1-936828-39-5

CONTENTS

REMARKS ON SOUPS. 11
    Soup Stock 11
    To make Beef Stock 12
    Veal Stock 13
    Croutons 13
    Marrow Dumplings for Soups 13
    Glaze 13
    Artichoke Soup 14
    Asparagus Soup 14
    Barley Soup 14
    Beef Tea 15
    Bisque of Crabs 15
    Bisque of Lobster 16
    Bouille-abaisse 16
    Cauliflower Soup 16
    Chestnut Soup 17
    Chicken Broth for the Invalid 17
    Chicken Soup 17
    Chicken Soup, No. 2 18
    Clam Broth 18
    Clam Chowder 18
    Consommé 19
    Consommé Colbert 19
    Cream of Celery 19
    Cream of Rice 19
    Cream Soup 20
    Fish Chowder 20
    German Soup 20
    Giblet Soup 21
    Green Turtle Soup 21
    Gumbo Soup 22
    Julienne Soup 23
    Lentil Soup 23
    Liebig's Soup 23
    Macaroni Soup 23
    Mock Turtle Soup 24
    Mulligatawny Soup 24
    Mutton Broth 25

Onion Soup 25
Oxtail Soup 25
Oyster Soup 26
Pea Soup 26
Pea Soup, Economical 26
Potato Soup 27
Purée of Beans 27
Purée of Clams 27
Rabbit Soup 28
Scotch Broth 28
Sorrel Soup 28
Spring Soup 29
Tomato Soup 29
Turkey Soup 29
Vegetable Soup 29
Vermicelli Soup 30

Recipes - PART 2 - Soups 31
  ALL ABOUT SOUPS 31
    VALUE OF SOUP IN THE MEAL 31
    GENERAL CLASSES OF SOUP 31
    CLASSES OF SOUP DENOTING CONSISTENCY 32
    CLASSES OF SOUPS DENOTING QUALITY 32
    STOCK FOR SOUP AND ITS USES 33
    VARIETIES OF STOCK 34
    ADDITIONAL USES OF STOCK 35
    SOUP EXTRACTS 35
    THE STOCK POT - NATURE, USE, AND CARE OF STOCK POT. 35
    FLAVORING STOCK 36
    MAKING OF SOUP 37
    PRINCIPAL INGREDIENTS 37
    MEAT USED FOR SOUP MAKING 37
    HERBS AND VEGETABLES USED FOR SOUP MAKING ... 39
    PROCESSES INVOLVED IN MAKING STOCK 39
    COOKING MEAT FOR SOUP 40
    REMOVING GREASE FROM SOUP 41
    CLEARING SOUP 41
    THICKENING SOUP 42
    SERVING SOUP 43

RECIPES – STOCKS 44
    WHITE STOCK 44
    BROWN SOUP STOCK 44
    VEGETABLE STOCK. 44
    FISH STOCK -1 45
    FISH STOCK -2 45
    STOCK FROM BONES -1 45
    STOCK FROM BONES -2 46
    VEAL STOCK 46
    BEEF STOCK -1 46
    BEEF STOCK -2 47
    SCOTCH MUTTON BROTH 47
    SCOTCH BROTH 47
    CREAM SOUP STOCK 48
    BRAN STOCK 48
    BARLEY BROTH 49
    STOCK FOR CLEAR SOUP OR BOUILLON 49
    CONSOMME 50
RECIPES - SOUPS 51
    ASPARAGUS SOUP 51
    ASPARAGUS CREAM 51
    APPLE SOUP -1 52
    ARTICHOKE SOUP 52
    BEEF SOUP 53
    BEAN SOUP 53
    BAKED BEAN SOUP 54
    BEAN AND CORN SOUP 54
    BEAN AND HOMINY SOUP 54
    BEAN AND POTATO SOUP 54
    BEAN AND TOMATO SOUP 55
    BISQUE SOUP 55
    BLACK BEAN SOUP 56
    BROWN SOUP 56
    BROWN MACARONI SOUP 57
    BARLEY SOUP 57
    BREAD SOUP 58
    BUTTER BEAN SOUP 58
    CABBAGE SOUP 59
    CABBAGE AND BACON SOUP 59
    CAPER SOUP 60

CARROT SOUP	60
CALF'S HEAD SOUP	61
CAULIFLOWER SOUP	61
CATFISH SOUP	62
COCOANUT SOUP	62
CORN SOUP	62
CLEAR SOUP	63
CLEAR SOUP WITH DUMPLINGS	63
CLEAR CELERY SOUP	63
CLEAR TOMATO SOUP	64
CREAM OF TOMATO SOUP	64
CREAM PEA SOUP	64
CREAM BARLEY SOUP	65
CREAM OF CELERY SOUP	65
CREAM OF RICE SOUP	65
CREAM OF ONION SOUP	65
CHICKEN SOUP	66
CHICKEN CREAM SOUP	66
CHICKEN CHEESE SOUP	66
CHEESE SOUP	67
CLAM SOUP	67
CHESTNUT SOUP	68
CHESTNUT PUREE	68
CANNED GREEN PEA SOUP	68
CANNED CORN SOUP	69
CELERY SOUP	69
CODFISH SOUP	69
COMBINATION SOUP	70
CURRY RICE SOUP	70
CROUTONS FOR SOUP	70
DRIED BEAN SOUP	70
DRIED WHITE BEANS SOUP	71
EEL SOUP	71
EGG SOUP	71
EGG BALLS FOR SOUP	72
EGG DUMPLINGS FOR SOUP	72
FISH SOUP	72
FISH CHOWDER	72
FRENCH SOUP	73
FRENCH CABBAGE SOUP	73

FRENCH ONION SOUP 73
FORCEMEAT BALLS FOR SOUP 73
GREEN CORN SOUP. 74
GREEN PEA SOUP 74
GREEN PEAS SOUP 74
GREEN BEAN SOUP 75
GREEN TURTLE SOUP 75
GROUSE SOUP 76
GIBLET SOUP 76
GUMBO SOUP 77
HARICOT SOUP 77
HARICOT BEAN SOUP 77
ITALIAN SOUP 78
IRISH POTATO SOUP 78
JULIENNE SOUP 78
KIDNEY SOUP 79
KORNLET SOUP 79
KORNLET AND TOMATO SOUP. 79
LENTIL SOUP 79
LENTIL AND PARSNIP SOUP 80
LETTUCE SOUP 80
LENTEN SOUP 80
LIMA BEAN SOUP 80
LEEK SOUP 81
LOBSTER SOUP 81
LOBSTER SOUP WITH MILK 81
MACARONI SOUP. 82
MILK SOUP 82
MILK SOUP FOR CHILDREN 82
MUSHROOM SOUP. 82
MULLIGATAWNY SOUP 83
MEAT BALLS FOR SOUP 83
NOODLE SOUP 83
NOODLES FOR SOUP 84
ONION SOUP 84
OATMEAL SOUP 84
OKRA SOUP 85
OX-TAIL SOUP 85
OYSTER SOUP 85
OYSTER SOUP -2 86

PARSNIP SOUP -1.	86
PARSNIP SOUP -2.	86
PEA AND TOMATO SOUP	87
PEAS SOUP	87
PEARS SOUP	87
PLUM SOUP	88
POTATO SOUP -1.	88
POTATO SOUP -2.	88
POTATO SOUP -3.	89
POTATO CHOWDER	89
POTATO AND RICE SOUP	89
POTATO AND VERMICELLI SOUP	89
PLAIN RICE SOUP	90
PEA SOUP -1.	90
PEA SOUP -2.	90
PHILADELPHIA PEPPER POT	91
PHILADELPHIA CLAM SOUP	91
PORTUGUESE SOUP	91
PUMPKIN SOUP	92
RICE SOUP	92
RICE CHEESE SOUP	92
RICE AND GREEN-PEA SOUP	92
RICE AND ONION SOUP	92
ST. ANDREW'S SOUP	93
SCARLET RUNNER SOUP	93
SORREL SOUP -1.	93
SORREL SOUP -2.	93
SPANISH SOUP -1	94
SPINACH SOUP -2	94
SPINACH CREAM	94
SPRING SOUP	95
SPRING VEGETABLE SOUP	95
SUMMER SOUP	95
SAGO SOUP	95
SAGO AND POTATO SOUP	96
SEMOLINA SOUP	96
SPLIT PEA SOUP -1.	96
SPLIT PEA SOUP -2.	96
SPLIT PEA PUREE	97
SWISS POTATO SOUP	97

SWISS LENTIL SOUP.. 97
SWISS WHITE SOUP.. 97
SUET DUMPLINGS FOR SOUP 98
SQUIRREL SOUP 98
TOMATO SOUP -1.. 98
TOMATO SOUP -2.. 99
TOMATO AND MACARONI SOUP... 99
TOMATO CREAM SOUP.. 99
TOMATO AND OKRA SOUP 100
TOMATO AND VERMICELLI SOUP 100
TAPIOCA AND TOMATO SOUP.. 100
TAPIOCA CREAM SOUP 100
TURNIP SOUP 101
TURKEY SOUP.. 101
TURTLE SOUP FROM BEANS. 101
VEGETABLE SOUP -1. 101
VEGETABLE SOUP -2. 102
VEGETABLE SOUP -3. 102
VEGETABLE MARROW SOUP. 102
VEGETABLE OYSTER SOUP -1 102
VEGETABLE OYSTER SOUP -2 103
VELVET SOUP... 103
VERMICELLI SOUP -1 103
VERMICELLI SOUP -2.. 103
VERMICELLI SOUP -3. 104
VEAL SOUP 104
WINTER VEGETABLE SOUP... 104
WHITE CELERY SOUP 104
WHITE SOUP 105
WHITE ONION SOUP... 105
WHOLEMEAL SOUP.. 105

REMARKS ON SOUPS

Soups, like salads, present an excellent opportunity for the cook to display good taste and judgment.

The great difficulty lies in selecting the most appropriate soup for each particular occasion; it would be well to first select your bill of fare, after which decide upon the soup.

The season, and force of circumstances, may compel you to decide upon a heavy fish, such as salmon, trout, or other oleaginous fishes, and heavy joints and entrées.

Under these circumstances it must necessarily follow that a light soup should begin the dinner, and *vice versa*; for large parties, one light and one heavy soup is always in order.

There is as much art in arranging a bill of fare and harmonizing the peculiarities of the various dishes, as there is in preparing the colors for a painting; the soup represents the pivot upon which harmony depends.

Soups may be divided into four classes: clear, thick, purées or bisques, and chowders. A purée is made by rubbing the cooked ingredients through a fine sieve; an ordinary thick soup is made by adding various thickening ingredients to the soup stock; clear soups are, properly speaking, the juices of meats, served in a convenient and appetizing form.

Chowders are quite distinct from the foregoing, being compounds of an infinite variety of fish, flesh, fowl, or vegetables, in proportions to suit the fluctuating ideas of the cook; the object sought is to prepare a thick, highly seasoned compound, without reducing the ingredients to the consistency of a purée.

Soup Stock

The word stock when used in cooking means the foundation or basis upon which soups and sauces depend; it is therefore the most important part of soup making. Care should be exercised that nothing in the least tainted or decayed enters the stock pot; it is very desirable that soup stock be prepared a day or two before it is wanted; the seasoning should be added in moderation at first, as it is difficult to restore a soup that has been damaged by over seasoning.

Milk or cream should be boiled and strained and added hot when intended for soups; when eggs are used beat them thoroughly, and add while the soup is hot. Should they be added when the soup is boiling, they are very apt to separate, and give the soup the appearance of having curdled; the best plan is to beat up the egg with a little of the warm soup, then add it to the soup gradually.

In summer, soup stock should be boiled from day to day, if kept any length of time, else it may become sour: should this happen, add a piece of charcoal to the soup, boil, cool, and strain into freshly scalded earthen or porcelain-lined ware. On no account allow the soup stock to become cold in an iron pot or saucepan.

To make Beef Stock

Take six pounds of soup meat, cut it up into good sized pieces, break the bones into small pieces, place them in the stock pot, and add five quarts of cold water and two ounces of salt; boil slowly for five hours, remove the scum as fast as it rises; cut up three white turnips and three carrots, add these to the soup with two stalks of celery, one large onion quartered, six cloves, teaspoonful of whole peppers, and a small bunch of herbs.

When the vegetables are thoroughly cooked, strain the soup into a large saucepan, and set it on back of range to keep hot, but not to boil, cut one pound of lean raw beef into fine pieces, put in into a saucepan, and add the whites and shells of four eggs; season with salt, pepper, and a little chopped parsley or celery tops; squeeze these together with your hand for fifteen minutes, until they are thoroughly incorporated, then add to the warm soup; allow the soup to simmer slowly one hour; taste for seasoning; strain into crocks, or serve. This is now called consommé or bouillon, and is the basis of nearly all soups; such items as macaroni, sago, Italian paste, Macedoine, and, in fact, nearly all kinds of cereals and soup ingredients may be added to this stock at different times to produce variety; they should all be boiled separately before adding to the soup.

Calf's feet and knuckle of veal may be added to the original or first pot if a very strong stock is required.

Veal Stock

Chop up three slices of bacon and two pounds of the neck of veal; place in a stew pan with a pint of water or beef stock, and simmer for half an hour; then add two quarts of stock, one onion, a carrot, a bouquet of herbs, four stalks of celery, half a teaspoonful of bruised whole peppers, and a pinch of nutmeg with a teaspoonful of salt; boil gently for two hours, removing the scum in the meantime. Strain into an earthen crock, and when cold remove the fat. A few bones of poultry added, with an additional quantity of water or stock, will improve it.

Croutons

Croutons or fried bread crumbs for soups, are prepared in this way:— Cut slices of stale home-made bread half an inch thick, trim off all crust and cut each slice into squares; fry these in very hot fat; drain them on a clean napkin, and add six or eight to each portion of soup.

Marrow Dumplings for Soups

Grate the crust of a breakfast roll, and break the remainder into crumbs; soak these in cold milk; drain, and add two ounces of flour; chop up half a pound of beef marrow freed from skin and sinews; beat up the yolks of five eggs; mix all together thoroughly, if too moist add some of the grated crumbs; salt and pepper to taste; form into small round dumplings; boil them in the soup for half an hour before serving.

Glaze

Glaze is made from rich soup stock, boiled down until it forms a dark, strong jelly. It is used in coloring soups and sauces and for glazing entrées. It should be kept in a stone crock.

Artichoke Soup

Melt a piece of butter the size of an egg in a saucepan; then fry in it one white turnip sliced, one red onion sliced, three pounds of Jerusalem artichokes washed, pared, and sliced, and a rasher of bacon. Stir these in the boiling butter for about ten minutes, add gradually one pint of stock. Let all boil together until the vegetables are thoroughly cooked, then add three pints more of stock; stir it well; add pepper and salt to taste, strain and press the vegetables through a sieve, and add one pint of boiling milk. Boil for five minutes more and serve.

Asparagus Soup

Take seventy-five heads of asparagus; cut away the hard, tough part, and boil the rest until tender. Drain them, and throw half into cold water until the soup is nearly ready, and press the other half through a hair sieve. Stir the pressed asparagus into two pints of stock, and let it boil; add salt, pepper, and a small lump of sugar. Cut the remaining heads of asparagus into peas; put them into the soup, and in a few minutes serve. If necessary color with a little spinach green.

Barley Soup

Put into a stock pot a knuckle of veal and two pounds of shoulder of mutton chopped up; cover with one gallon of cold water; season with salt, whole peppers, and a blade of mace; boil for three hours, removing the scum as fast as it rises. Wash half a pint of barley in cold water, drain and cover it with milk, and let it stand for half an hour, drain and add to the soup; boil half an hour longer, moderately; strain, trim the meat from the bone, chop up a little parsley or celery tops, add a tablespoonful to the soup and serve.

Beef Tea

Take half a pound of lean beef; cut it up into small bits; let it soak in a pint of water for three-quarters of an hour; then put both into a quart champagne bottle with just a suspicion of salt. Cork tightly, and wire the cork, so as to prevent its popping out. Set the bottle in a saucepan full of warm water, boil gently for an hour and a half, and strain through a napkin. Beef tea, without the fibrine of the meat, if administered often to a patient, will tend to weaken, instead of strengthening the invalid; always add about a teaspoonful of finely chopped raw meat to a goblet of the tea, and let it stand in the tea for about five minutes before serving.

Bisque of Crabs

Boil twelve hard-shell crabs for thirty minutes, and drain; when cold break them apart, pick out the meat carefully, scrape off all fat adhering to the upper shell, and save these for deviled crabs (an excellent recipe for deviled crabs may be found in "Salads and Sauces.")

Set the crab meat aside; put the under shell and the claws in a mortar with half a pound of butter and a cupful of cold boiled rice, and pound them as smooth as possible; then put this into a saucepan, and add a heaping teaspoonful of salt, a bouquet of assorted herbs, a dozen whole peppers, a blade of mace, and three quarts of stock; boil slowly for one hour, pour it through a sieve, and work as much of the pulp through the sieve as possible. Place the soup on the range to keep warm, but not to boil.

Beat up the yolk of one egg, and add it slowly to a quart of warm milk previously boiled; whisk the milk into the soup; taste for seasoning. Now take the crab meat and heat it in a little boiling water, drain, put it into a hot soup tureen, pour the soup over it and serve.

Bisque of Lobster

Procure two large live lobsters; chop them up while raw, shells and all; put them into a mortar with three-fourths of a pound of butter, three raw eggs, and one quarter of a pound of cold boiled rice: pound to a paste, moisten with a little water or stock, then set aside. Fry out two slices of bacon fat, add to it one minced onion, a tablespoonful of chopped celery tops, one chopped long red pepper, one sliced carrot, and a quart of stock, boil and pour the whole into a saucepan. Add the lobster and three pints more of stock; boil slowly for two hours; strain, and rub the ingredients through a sieve. Return to the soup; keep it warm, but do not allow it to boil. If too thick, add a little more stock; add salt to taste. Boil one quart of cream; whisk it into the soup; taste again for seasoning; pour it into a hot soup tureen, and send to table.This soup can be prepared by following receipt for bisque of crab, or it may be prepared by adding boiled lobster to a strong veal stock, and colored red by pounding the coral with butter, and adding this to the soup.

Bouille-abaisse

Take six pounds of cod-fish; cut it up into small pieces; chop two red onions; put them in a stew pan with an ounce of butter; let them brown without burning. Now add the fish and four tablespoonfuls of fine olive-oil, a bruised clove of garlic, two bay leaves, four slices of lemon peeled and quartered, half a pint of Shrewsbury tomato catsup, and half a salt-spoonful of saffron. Add sufficient hot soup stock to cover the whole; boil slowly for half to three-quarters of an hour; skim carefully while boiling; when ready to serve add a tablespoonful of chopped celery tops.

Cauliflower Soup

Fry half an onion in a very little butter; when it is a light brown add a tablespoonful of minced raw ham and two or three stalks of celery, then add a quart of soup stock; simmer slowly for half an hour. Boil for twenty-five or thirty minutes one medium-sized head of cauliflower in water slightly salted. Strain the contents of the frying-pan into a saucepan, and add one quart more of stock. Drain the cauliflower; rub it through a fine sieve into the stock; boil just once; draw to one side of the fire; taste for seasoning. Now dissolve a teaspoonful of rice flour in half a cupful of cold milk; whisk the soup thoroughly; pour into a hot tureen, and serve.

Chestnut Soup

Remove the outer peel or coating from twenty-five Italian chestnuts; pour scalding water over them, and rub off the inner coating. Put them into a saucepan with one quart of soup stock, and boil for three-quarters of an hours; drain; rub them through a colander, then through a sieve, with one tablespoonful of cracker dust, or pound to a paste in a mortar; season with salt and pepper; add gradually the stock in which they were boiled; add one pint more of stock; boil once, and draw to one side of the fire.

Beat up the yolks of two raw eggs; add them to one quart of warm milk; whisk the milk into the soup; taste for seasoning; pour into a hot tureen, and send to table with croutons.

Chicken Broth for the Invalid

Procure a dry-picked Philadelphia roasting chicken; cut it in halves; put one half in the ice box; chop the other half into neat pieces; put it into a small saucepan; add one quart of cold water, a little salt and a leaf of celery; simmer gently for two hours; remove the oily particles thoroughly; strain the broth into a bowl; when cooled a little, serve to the convalescent. Serve the meat with the broth.

Chicken Soup

Take three young male chickens; cut them up; put them in a saucepan with three quarts of veal stock. (A sliced carrot, one turnip, and one head of celery may be put with them and removed before the soup is thickened.) Let them simmer for an hour. Remove all the white flesh; return the rest of the birds to the soup, and boil gently for two hours. Pour a little of the liquid over a quarter of a pound of bread crumbs, and when they are well soaked put it in a mortar with the white flesh of the birds, and pound the whole to a smooth paste: add a pinch of ground mace, salt, and a little cayenne pepper; press the mixture through a sieve, and boil once more, adding a pint of boiling cream; thicken with a little flour mixed in cold milk; remove the bones, and serve.

Chicken Soup, No. 2

Cut up one chicken, put into a stewpan two quarts of cold water, a teaspoonful of salt, and one pod of red pepper; when half done add two desert spoonfuls of well washed rice: when thoroughly cooked, remove the bird from the soup, tear a part of the breast into shreds (saving the remainder of the fowl for a salad), and add it to the soup with a wine-glass full of cream.

Clam Broth

Procure three dozen little-neck clams in the shell; wash them well in cold water; put them in a saucepan, cover with a quart of hot water; boil fifteen minutes; drain; remove the shells; chop up the clams, and add them to the hot broth with a pat of butter; salt if necessary and add a little cayenne; boil ten minutes, pour into a soup tureen, add a slice of toast, and send to table. This is the mode adopted when we do not have a clam opener in the house.

Raw, freshly opened clams should be chopped fine and prepared in the manner above described. The large clams are better for chowders than for stews and broth.

Clam Chowder

Chop up fifty large clams; cut eight medium-sized potatoes into small square pieces, and keep them in cold water until wanted. Chop one large, red onion fine, and cut up half a pound of larding pork into small pieces. Procure an iron pot, and see that it is very clean and free from rust; set it on the range, and when very hot, throw the pieces of pork into it, fry them brown; next add the onion, and fry it brown; add one fourth of the chopped clams, then one fourth of the chopped potato, and two pilot crackers quartered, a teaspoonful of salt, one chopped, long, red pepper, a teaspoonful of powdered thyme and half a pint of canned tomato pulp. Repeat this process until the clams and potato are used, omitting the seasoning; add hot water enough to cover all, simmer slowly three hours. Should it become too thick, add more hot water; occasionally remove the pot from the range, take hold of the handle, and twist the pot round several times; this is done to prevent the chowder from burning. On no account disturb the chowder with a spoon or ladle until done; now taste for seasoning, as it is much easier to season properly after the chowder is cooked than before. A few celery tops may be added if desired.

Consommé

This is nothing more than beef stock, with a little more attention given to clarifying it. It is always acceptable if the dinner to follow is composed of heavy joints and side dishes. If the party consists of more than twenty, serve one thick soup and one light soup or consommé.

Consommé Colbert

Prepare a strong consommé; add to two quarts of it a tablespoonful each of shredded young turnips and carrots and a tablespoonful of green peas; simmer until the vegetables are tender; taste for seasoning.

Poach four eggs in hot water in the usual manner; send these to table with the soup. In serving add one poached egg to each plate. It is well always to poach two extra eggs to be used should any of the others be broken in the service.

Cream of Celery

Cut up six stalks of celery into half-inch pieces; put them into a saucepan with one red onion quartered, one blade of mace, salt, and a few whole peppers; add a quart of veal stock, and boil for one hour. Rub the ingredients through a sieve; put the pulp into a saucepan, and add one quart more of veal stock; boil; then draw to one side of fire to keep hot. Boil three pints of cream; strain it into the soup; whisk the soup at the same time (if not thick enough to suit your taste add a little flour); taste for seasoning; pour it into a hot tureen; serve with small pieces of toast or croutons.

Cream of Rice

Wash thoroughly a half pound of rice; pick out all imperfect or colored grains; put it into a saucepan and add two quarts of stock. Boil slowly for one hour; then rub the rice through a sieve twice; return it to the stock; season with salt and pepper. Care must be exercised that the rice does not adhere to the bottom of the saucepan. Simmer until wanted. Beat up the yolks of two eggs; add them slowly to a quart of warm, milk previously boiled; whisk the milk into the soup, which must not be very hot; then pour it into a hot tureen, and serve.

Cream Soup

Prepare two quarts of strong veal stock; set it on the back part of the range to simmer.

Boil one quart of cream; whisk it into the stock; pour it into a hot tureen, and serve with croutons. If convenient the breast of a boiled chicken may be added.

Fish Chowder

Take two fine, fresh cod-fish, weighing six pounds each; clean them well; cut the fish lengthwise from the bone, and cut it into pieces two inches square. Chop up the bones and heads; put them into a saucepan; add three quarts of warm water, one red onion sliced, heaping teaspoonful of salt, a dozen bruised peppercorns, and a few stalks of celery. Boil until the fish drops from the bones; then strain into another saucepan.

Cut into small squares one peck of small potatoes and a pound and a half of salt pork; arrange the fish, pork, and potatoes into mounds; divide each equally into four parts; add one quarter of the fish to the stock, next a quarter of the pork, then a quarter of the potato, and three pilot crackers, broken into quarters, salt, pepper, and a little thyme. Repeat this process until the remaining three quarters of pork, fish, and potato, are used; cover all with warm milk; simmer slowly until the fish is tender, care being taken that the soup does not boil over; now taste for seasoning, serve as neatly as possible.

The above is the old-fashioned New England fish chowder. Clams may be used instead of fish.

German Soup

Melt half an ounce of fresh butter in a saucepan; when very hot, add half an onion, chopped fine, and a teaspoonful of caraway seeds. When the onion is slightly browned, add three quarts of strong veal stock, well seasoned; simmer gently for three quarters of an hour. Prepare some marrow dumplings; boil them in water, or a portion of the soup, and serve.

Giblet Soup

An economical, and at the same time excellent, soup, is made from the legs, neck, heart, wings, and gizzard of all kinds of poultry. These odds and ends are usually plentiful about the holidays.

To turn them to account, follow general instructions for chicken soup; add a little rice, and your soup is complete.

Green Turtle Soup

Many housewives imagine that green turtle is too expensive, and too difficult to prepare for household use, and for these reasons it is seldom met with in private families, except in tin cans. Even this is not always made from turtle.

This soup is not any more expensive than many other kinds. A small turtle may be purchased at Fulton market for from ten to twenty cents per pound, and weighing from fifteen to forty pounds, the price varying according to the law of supply and demand. The only objection to small turtles is that they do not contain a very large percentage of the green fat, so highly prized by epicures.

Procure a live turtle, cut off the head, and allow it to drain and cool over night; next morning place it on the working table, lay it on its back, and make an incision round the inner edge of the shell; then remove it. Now remove the intestines carefully, and be very careful that you do not break the gall; throw these away; cut off the fins and all fleshy particles, and set them aside; trim out the fat, which has a blueish tint when raw; wash it well in several waters. Chop up the upper and under shells with a cleaver; put them with the fins into a large saucepan; cover them with boiling water; let stand ten minutes; drain and rub off the horny, scaly particles, with a kitchen towel.

Scald a large saucepan, and put all the meat and shell into it (except the fat); cover with hot water; add a little salt, and boil four hours. Skim carefully, and drain; put the meat into a large crock; remove the bones, and boil the fat in the stock. This does not take very long if first scalded. When done, add it also to the crock; pour the stock into another crock; let it cool, and remove all scum and oily particles; this is quite work enough for one day. Clean the saucepans used, and dry them thoroughly.

Next day fry out half a pound of fat ham; then add one chopped onion, one bay leaf, six cloves, one blade of mace, two tablespoonfuls of chopped celery tops, a tablespoonful of salt, a teaspoonful of white pepper, and one quart of ordinary soup stock. Simmer for half an hour. Now put the turtle stock on the fire; when hot strain the seasoning into it; remove the turtle from the other crock, cut it up, and add to the stock; now add a pint of dry sherry.

Do not let the soup come to a boil; taste for seasoning, and if herbs are needed tie a string to a bunch of mixed herbs, throw them into the soup, and tie the other end to the saucepan handle; taste often, and when palatable, remove the herbs. If the soup is not dark enough, brown a very little flour and add to it. Keep the soup quite hot until served; add quartered slices of lemon and the yolk of a hard boiled egg, quartered just before serving; send to table with a decanter of sherry.

The yolks of the eggs may be worked to a paste, and made into round balls to imitate turtle eggs if this is desired.

I have placed before my readers this complicated receipt in as simple a form as it is possible to do, having carefully avoided all the technical formulas used in the profession.

Gumbo Soup

Cut up two chickens, two slices of ham, and two onions into dice; flour them, and fry the whole to a light brown; then fill the frying pan with boiling water; stir it a few minutes, and turn the whole into a saucepan containing three quarts of boiling water. Let it boil for forty minutes, removing the scum.

In the meantime soak three pints of ochra in cold water for twenty minutes; cut them into thin slices, and add to the other ingredients; let it boil for one hour and a half. Add a quart of canned tomatoes and a cupful of boiled rice half an hour before serving.

Julienne Soup

Cut into fine shreds, an inch long, two carrots, two turnips, two heads of celery, and the white ends of two spring leeks. Put them into a frying pan, with one ounce of butter, a teaspoonful of salt, and one lump of cut sugar; simmer until tender, then add a cupful of stock. Put two quarts of veal stock in a saucepan; add the vegetables, and a teaspoonful of chopped parsley, a little fresh sorrel if convenient (wild wood sorrel is the best for julienne) shredded. Taste for seasoning; boil once, and serve.

Lentil Soup

Lentils are very nutritious, and form the basis of a most excellent soup; but they are little used in American cookery. Soak a pint of dry lentils for two hours; put them in a saucepan; add two quarts of cold water, half an onion, two or three celery tops, salt, whole peppers, and two or three ounces of the small end of a ham. Boil gently for three hours; add a little more hot water, if the quantity has been reduced by boiling, pour through a sieve, remove the ham, onion and celery; rub the lentils through a sieve, return to the soup; whisk it thoroughly; taste for seasoning, and serve with croutons.

Liebig's Soup

An excellent soup may be prepared at short notice, as follows:—Take half an onion, three or four outer stocks of celery, one carrot sliced, salt, pepper, and a very little mace. Boil these in two quarts of water for half an hour; strain, and add to the water two tablespoonfuls of Liebig's Extract of meat; whisk thoroughly, taste for seasoning, and serve.

Macaroni Soup

Boil half a pound of Macaroni for half an hour, in three pints of water slightly salted; add a blade of mace. When done, drain, and cut it into two inch pieces. Put three pints of soup stock into a saucepan; add the macaroni; taste for seasoning, boil a moment and serve.

Mock Turtle Soup

Take half a calf's head, with the skin on; remove the brains. Wash the head in several waters, and let it soak in cold water for an hour. Put it in a saucepan with five quarts of beef stock; let it simmer gently for an hour; remove the scum carefully. Take up the head and let it get cold; cut the meat from the bones into pieces an inch square, and set them in the ice-box.

Dissolve two ounces of butter in a frying pan; mince a large onion, and fry it in the butter until nicely browned, and add to the stock in which the head was cooked. Return the bones to the stock; simmer the soup, removing the scum until no more rises. Put in a carrot, a turnip, a bunch of parsley, a bouquet of herbs, a dozen outer stalks of celery, two blades of mace and the rind of one lemon, grated; salt and pepper to taste. Boil gently for two hours, and strain the soup through a cloth. Mix three ounces of browned flour with a pint of the soup; let simmer until it thickens, then add it to the soup. Take the pieces of head out of the ice-box, and add to the soup; let them simmer until quite tender. "Before serving add a little Worcestershire sauce, a tablespoonful of anchovy paste, a gobletful of port or sherry, and two lemons sliced, each slice quartered, with the rind trimmed off." Warm the wine a very little before adding it to the soup. Keep in ice-box three or four days before using. Serve the brains as a side dish.

Mulligatawny Soup

Divide a large chicken into neat pieces; take a knuckle of veal, and chop it up; put all into a large saucepan, and add one gallon of water; salt; boil for three hours or until reduced one-third. Put an ounce of butter in a hot frying pan, cut up two red onions, and fry them in the butter. Into a half pint of the stock put two heaping tablespoonfuls of curry powder; add this to the onion, then add the whole to the soup, now taste for seasoning. Some like a little wine, but these are the exception and not the rule. Before serving add half a slice of lemon to each portion. Many prefer a quantity of rice to be added to the soup before it is finished; the rice should be first well washed and parboiled.

Mutton Broth

Take four pounds of lean mutton trimmings; cut them into neat pieces; put them into a saucepan; add three quarts of cold water, one heaping teaspoonful of salt. Bruise, and add six peppercorns, three or four celery tops, and one young leek. Boil slowly for two hours; remove the scum as it rises. Boil a cupful of rice for twenty minutes; add it to the soup, and taste for seasoning; remove the celery, leek, and mutton bones; pour the soup into a hot tureen, and serve.

Substitute a knuckle of veal for mutton, and you will have an excellent veal broth.

Onion Soup

Peel and cut into small pieces three medium-sized onions; fry them in a little butter until tender, but not brown; pour over them a pint of stock; add a little salt and cayenne. Simmer for fifteen minutes; press the soup through a sieve; put it in a saucepan, and add three tablespoonfuls of grated bread crumbs, and half a gobletful of hot cream. Taste for seasoning, and serve with small slices of toast.

Oxtail Soup

Take two oxtails; cut them into joints, and cut each joint into four pieces; put them into a pan with two ounces of butter, and fry them for ten minutes. Slice two onions, one turnip, two carrots, and a dozen outer stalks of celery, and fry in the same butter, with three slices of bacon cut up fine; fry to a light brown. Turn the ingredients into a saucepan with a quart of stock or ham water, and boil quickly for half an hour, then add two more quarts of stock, a bouquet of herbs, two bay-leaves, a dozen whole peppers crushed, a few cloves, and salt to taste. Simmer until the meat is quite tender; then take it out; strain the soup; skim off the fat, and thicken with two ounces of flour. Return the meat to the soup; add a tablespoonful of Worcestershire, and a cupful of sherry, and serve with grated rusks.

Oyster Soup

Wet a saucepan with cold water; pour into it two quarts of milk. When at boiling point, add two dozen oysters and a pint of oyster liquor well seasoned with salt and pepper. Dissolve a tablespoonful of rice flour in a little cold milk; finally add a large tablespoonful of table butter; do not let the soup boil again as it will contract the oysters. Pour into a tureen, taste for salting, and serve, a few broken crackers may be added. The object in wetting the pan is to prevent the milk from burning.

Pea Soup

Cut two large slices of ham into dice, with a sliced onion, and fry them in a little bacon fat until they are lightly browned. Cut up one turnip, one large carrot, four outer stalks of celery, and one leek into small pieces; add these last ingredients to the ham and onion, and let them simmer for fifteen minutes; then pour over them three quarts of corned-beef water or hot water, and add a pint of split peas which have been soaked in cold water over night.

Boil gently until the peas are quite tender stirring constantly to prevent burning; then add salt and pepper to taste, and a teaspoonful of brown sugar. Remove the soup from the fire, and rub through a sieve; if it is not thick enough to suit your taste, add a few ounces of flour mixed smoothly in a little cold milk; return the soup to the fire, and simmer for half an hour. Cut up four slices of American bread into small dice, and fry the pieces in very hot fat until nicely browned; place them on a napkin or towel, and add a few to each plate or tureen of soup just before it goes to table.

Pea Soup, Economical

Boil for four hours two quarts of green pea hulls in four quarts of water, in which beef, mutton, or fowl has been boiled, then add a bunch or bouquet of herbs, salt and pepper, a teaspoonful of butter, and a quart of milk. Rub through a hair sieve, thicken with a little flour, and serve with croutons, as in the foregoing receipt.

Potato Soup

Wash and peel two dozen small sized potatoes; put them into a saucepan with two onions; add three quarts of corned-beef water; boil for one hour and a half until the potatoes fall to pieces. Pour the soup through a sieve, and rub the potato through it to a fine pulp; put the whole into the saucepan again; when very hot add a pint of hot rich cream, salt and pepper, if necessary; whisk thoroughly; pour into a tureen, add croutons, and serve.

Purée of Beans

Soak two quarts of small, white beans over night; change the water twice; drain, put them into a pot or saucepan, and cover them with cold water. Boil slowly for six hours; as the water evaporates, add hot water. One hour before the beans are cooked add one pound of salt pork, a bunch of fresh herbs, half a dozen whole cloves, salt if necessary; when done pour the soup through a sieve, remove the pork and seasoning, and rub the soup through a sieve; add the pulp to the stock; taste for seasoning; pour the soup into a tureen, add croutons and serve. Many prefer a ham bone to pork.

Purée of Clams

Chop twenty-five large hard-shell clams, very fine, and put them aside; fry half a chopped red onion in an ounce of hot butter; add a teaspoonful of chopped celery tops, a blade of mace, one salted anchovy, six whole peppers, and a pint of soup stock. Let it boil; then strain into a saucepan; add the chopped clams and one quart of stock or hot water. Boil slowly one hour; strain all the clams through a sieve twice, and return to the stock; season with salt and cayenne. Keep the soup warm, but do not let it boil again; taste for seasoning. Boil one pint of cream in a saucepan previously wet with cold water; strain it, and add to the soup slowly. Mix a teaspoonful of rice flour in a little cold milk; add to the soup; whisk the soup; taste again for seasoning; pour it into a hot tureen, and serve.

Rabbit Soup

Cut up two jack rabbits into neat pieces; put them into a stew pan containing one quarter of a pound of melted butter; add a slice of fat bacon cut into small pieces. Fry for five minutes in the butter; slice two small carrots, and two red onions, and add to the saucepan with one bay leaf, one blade of mace, four cloves, a few green celery stalks, one ounce of salt, and one long red pepper.

Pour over all, one gallon of stock; simmer gently for nearly three hours; skim carefully; strain into a saucepan, and set on back of range to keep hot, but not to boil. Add half a pint of dry sherry, and serve with croutons. If not dark enough add a little glaze.

Scotch Broth

Take two pounds of mutton trimmings; cut into neat pieces; put into a saucepan with three quarts of water, one large red onion, salt, and a dozen whole peppers. Boil gently, and remove the scum as it rises; wash half a pint of barley; soak it while the soup is boiling, and add it at the end of the first hour. Let the soup boil for two hours longer; taste for seasoning; pour slowly into a soup tureen, leaving the meat in the saucepan. Some prefer to take the meat out of the soup, and after removing the bones they return the meat to the soup.

Sorrel Soup

Sorrel is an excellent ingredient for soup. Its acid leaves are much appreciated by the French; the wild sorrel may be used, but now that truck gardeners are cultivating it extensively, it will be found less troublesome to use the latter.

The Germans make the best sorrel soup; their recipe is as follows:—Wash and pick over two quarts of sorrel; remove the stems; then cut the sorrel into pieces. Heat two ounces of butter in a small saucepan; add the sorrel and a few blades of chives; cover without water and allow it to steam for half an hour. Stir to prevent burning; sprinkle over this a tablespoonful of flour free from lumps. Now add three quarts of well-seasoned veal stock; taste for seasoning; boil once, and send to table with croutons or small bits of toast. This is an excellent spring and summer soup.

Spring Soup

Take two quarts of nicely seasoned veal stock; place it on the range to keep hot, but not to boil. Cut into neat strips four young carrots, four young spring turnips, and two spring leeks; add them to the stock. Now add half a pint of fresh green peas; boil gently for fifteen minutes; taste for seasoning, and serve.

Tomato Soup

Cut four ounces of ham into dice; slice two onions, and fry with ham in two ounces of butter; when browned turn them into a saucepan containing three quarts of stock or corned-beef water, and add three carrots, two turnips, and one long red pepper, and a dozen outer stalks of celery. Simmer gently for one hour; then add a quart of canned tomatoes; boil gently for another hour; rub the whole through a sieve, and simmer again with the liquor a few minutes; add salt, and serve with fried bread crumbs.

Turkey Soup

Take the remains of a cold roast turkey, trim off all the meat, break up the bones, and put them into a saucepan; cover them with two quarts of veal stock; salt and cayenne to taste. Boil gently for one hour; strain and skim. Now add the flesh of the turkey; simmer gently; dissolve a tablespoonful of rice flour in a little cold milk, and add it to the soup. Let it come to a boil; taste for seasoning, and serve with croutons.

Vegetable Soup

Wash and clean two carrots and two turnips; cut them into slices, and cut each slice into small narrow strips; put them into a saucepan with four stalks of celery cut into inch pieces, a dozen button onions, one long red pepper, and a teaspoonful of salt; add three quarts of soup stock; boil until the vegetables are tender, add a lump of sugar, and serve. The carrots and turnips may be cut into fancy shapes with a vegetable cutter.

Vermicelli Soup

Take one quarter of a pound of vermicelli; break it into pieces, and boil it for five minutes; drain and add it to three pints of strong soup stock. Boil once; draw to one side, and simmer gently for twenty minutes. Should any scum arise, remove it; taste for seasoning, and send to table with a little Parmesan cheese.

Recipes - PART 2 - Soups

ALL ABOUT SOUPS

SOUP is a liquid food that is prepared by boiling meat or vegetables, or both, in water and then seasoning and sometimes thickening the liquid that is produced. It is usually served as the first course of a dinner, but it is often included in a light meal, such as luncheon. Soup is an easily made, economical, and when properly prepared from healthful and nutritious material, very wholesome article of diet, deserving of much more general use than is commonly accorded it.

The purpose of this Section is to acquaint you with the details of making appetizing and nutritious soups that make for both economy and healthfulness.

VALUE OF SOUP IN THE MEAL

Soup contains the very essence of all that is nourishing and sustaining in the foods of which it is made. The importance of soup is to consider the purposes it serves in a meal. When its variety and the ingredients of which it is composed are thought of, soup serves two purposes: first, as an appetizer taken at the beginning of a meal to stimulate the appetite and aid in the flow of digestive juices in the stomach; and secondly, as an actual part of the meal, when it must contain sufficient nutritive material to permit it to be considered as a part of the meal instead of merely an addition.

Care should be taken to make this food attractive enough to appeal to the appetite rather than discourage it. Soup should not be greasy nor insipid in flavor, neither should it be served in large quantities nor without proper accompaniment. A small quantity of well-flavored, attractively served soup cannot fail to meet the approval of any family when it is served as the first course of the meal.

GENERAL CLASSES OF SOUP

The two purposes for which soup is used have led to the placing of the numerous kinds into two general asses. In the first class are grouped those which serve as appetizers, such as bouillon, consomme, and some other broths and clear soups. In the second class are included those eaten for their nutritive effect, such as cream soups, purees, and bisques. From these two classes of soup, the one that will correspond with the rest of the meal and make it balance properly is the one to choose. For instance, a light soup that is merely an appetizer should be served with a heavy dinner, whereas a heavy, highly nutritious soup should be used with a luncheon or a light meal.

The two general classes of soup already mentioned permit of numerous methods of classification. For instance, soups are sometimes named from the principal ingredient or an imitation of it, as the names potato soup, beef soup, macaroni soup, mock-turtle soup testify. Again, both stimulating and nutritious soups may be divided into thin and thick soups, thin soups usually being clear, and thick soups, because of their nature, cloudy. When the quality of soups is considered, they are placed in still different classes and are called broth, bisque, consomme, puree, and so on. Another important classification of soups results from the nationality of the people who use them.

CLASSES OF SOUP DENOTING CONSISTENCY

As has already been pointed out, soups are of only two kinds when their consistency is thought of, namely, clear soups and thick soups.

CLEAR SOUPS are those made from carefully cleared stock, or soup foundation, and flavored or garnished with a material from which the soup usually takes its name. There are not many soups of this kind, bouillon and consomme being the two leading varieties, but in order to be palatable, they require considerable care in making.

THICK SOUPS are also made from stock, but milk or cream and any mixture of these may also be used as a basis and to it may be added for thickening meat, fish, vegetables, eggs, or grain or some other starchy material. Soups of this kind are often made too thick and as such soups are not appetizing, care must be taken to have them just right in consistency.

CLASSES OF SOUPS DENOTING QUALITY

When attention is given to the quality of soup, this food divides itself into several varieties, namely, broth, cream soup, bisque, chowder and puree.

BROTHS have for their foundation a clear stock. They are sometimes a thin soup, but other times they are made quite thick with vegetables, rice or barley when they are served as a substantial part of a meal.

CREAM SOUPS are highly nutritious and are of great variety. They have for their foundation a thin cream sauce, but to this are always added vegetables, meat, fish or grains.

BISQUES are thick, rich soups made from game fish or shell fish, particularly crabs, shrimp etc. occasionally, vegetables are used in soups of this kind.

CHOWDERS are soups that have sea food for their basis. Vegetables and crackers are generally added for thickening and to impart flavor.

PUREES are soups made thick partly or entirely by the addition of some material obtained by boiling an article of food and then straining it to form a pulp. When vegetables containing starch such as beans, peas, lentils or potatoes are used for this purpose, it is unnecessary to thicken the soup with any additional starch; but when meat, fish or watery vegetables are used, other thickening is required. To be right, a puree should be nearly as smooth as thick cream and of the same consistency.

STOCK FOR SOUP AND ITS USES

In order that soup-making processes may be readily grasped, one should be thoroughly familiar with what is meant by stock which forms the foundation of many soups. A stock of anything means a reserve supply of that thing stored away for future use. When applied to soup, stock is similar in meaning for it refers to material stored or prepared in such a way that it may be kept for use in the making of certain kinds of soup.

In a more definite sense, soup-stock may be regarded as a liquid containing the juices and soluble parts of meat, bone or vegetables which have been extracted by long, slow cooking.

Soups in which stock is utilized include all the varieties made from beef, veal, mutton and poultry. If clear stock is desired for the making of soup, only fresh meat and bones should be used and all material that will discolor the liquid in any way carefully avoided. For ordinary, unclarified soups, the trimmings and bones of roast, steak or chops and the carcass of fowl can generally be utilized. However, very strongly flavored meat such as mutton or the fat from mutton should be used sparingly.

VARIETIES OF STOCK

Several kinds of stock are utilized in the making of soup, and the kind to employ depends on the soup desired. The following classification will be a guide in determining the kind of stock required for the foundation of a soup.

FIRST STOCK is made from meat and bones and then clarified and used for well-flavored, clear soups.

SECOND STOCK is made from the meat and the bones that remain after the first stock is strained off. More water is added to the remaining material and this is then cooked with vegetables, which supply the needed flavor. Such stock serves very well for adding flavor to a nutritious soup made from vegetables or cereal foods.

WHITE STOCK is used in the preparation of white soups and is made by boiling six pounds of a knuckle of veal cut up in small pieces and poultry trimmings. Proceed according to directions given in STOCK.

HOUSEHOLD STOCK is made by cooking meat and bones, either fresh or cooked, with vegetables or other material that will impart flavor and add nutritive value. Stock of this kind is used for ordinary soups.

BONE STOCK is made from meat bones to which vegetables are added for flavor and it is used for making any of the ordinary soups.

VEGETABLE STOCK is made from either dried or fresh vegetables or both. Such stock is employed in making vegetable soups.

GAME STOCK is made from the bones and trimmings of game to which vegetables are added for flavor. This kind of stock is used for making game soups.

FISH STOCK is made from fish or fish trimmings to which vegetables are added for flavor. Shell fish make especially good stock of this kind. Fish stock is employed for making chowders and fish soups.

ADDITIONAL USES OF STOCK

As has already been shown, stock is used principally as a foundation for certain varieties of soup. This material, however, may be utilized in many other ways, being especially valuable in the use of leftover foods. Any bits of meat or fowl that are left over can be made into an appetizing dish by adding thickened stock to them and serving the combination over toast or rice. In fact, a large variety of made dishes can be devised if there is stock on hand to add for flavor. The convenience of a supply of stock will be apparent when it is realized that gravy or sauce for almost any purpose can be made from the contents of the stockpot.

SOUP EXTRACTS

If there is no time to go through the various processes involved in making soup, there are a number of concentrated meat and vegetable extracts on the market for making soups quickly. The meat extracts are made of the same flavoring material as that which is drawn from meat in the making of stock. Almost all the liquid is evaporated and the result is a thick, dark substance that must be diluted greatly with water to obtain the basis for a soup or a broth. Some of the vegetable extracts such as Japanese soy and English marmite are so similar in appearance and taste to the meat extracts as to make it quite difficult to detect any difference. Both varieties of these extracts may be used for sauces and gravies, as well as for soups, but it should be remembered that they are not highly nutritious and are valuable merely for flavoring.

THE STOCK POT - NATURE, USE, AND CARE OF STOCK POT.

Among the utensils used for cooking there is probably none more convenient and useful than the stockpot. It is nothing more or less than a covered crock or pot, into which materials that will make a well-flavored stock are put from time to time. From such a supply, stock can be drawn when it is needed for soup; then, when some is taken out, more water and materials may be added to replenish the pot. The stockpot should be made of either enamel or earthenware, since a metal pot of any kind is liable to impart flavor to the food.

The stock pot, like any other utensil used for making soup, should receive considerable care, as it must be kept scrupulously clean. No stock pot should ever be allowed to stand from day to day without being emptied, thoroughly washed, and then exposed to the air for a while to dry.

FLAVORING STOCK

It is the flavoring of stock that indicates real skill in soup making. This is an extremely important part of the work. In fact, the large number of ingredients found in soup recipes are, as a rule, the various flavorings which give the distinctive flavor and individuality to a soup. Very often certain spices or certain flavoring materials may be omitted without any appreciable difference, or something that is on hand may be substituted for an ingredient that is lacking.

The flavorings used most for soup include cloves, peppercorns, red, black and white pepper, paprika, bay leaf, sage, marjoram, thyme, summer savory, tarragon, celery seed, fennel, mint and rosemary. While all of these are not absolutely necessary, the majority of them may well be kept on the pantry shelf. A small amount of lemon peel often improves soup, so some of this should be kept in store. Another group of vegetables that lend themselves admirably to soup flavoring includes leeks, shallots, chives, garlic and onions, all of which belong to the same family. They must be used judiciously, as a strong flavor of any of them is offensive to most persons.

In the use of any of the flavorings mentioned or the strongly flavored vegetables, care should be taken not to allow any one particular flavor to predominate. Each should be used in such quantity that it would blend well with the others. A very good way in which to fix spices and herbs that are to flavor soup is to tie them in a small piece of cheesecloth and drop the bag thus made into the soup pot. When prepared in this way, they will remain together, so that, while the flavor can be cooked out, they can be more readily removed from the liquid than if they are allowed to spread through the contents of the pot. Salt should be added in the proportion of 1 teaspoonful to each quart of liquid.

MAKING OF SOUP

Always use soft water for making soup and be careful to proportion the quantity of water to that of the meat. Somewhat less than a quart of water to a pound of meat, is a good rule for common soups. Rich soups, intended for company, may have a still smaller allowance of water.

PRINCIPAL INGREDIENTS

The making of the stock that is used in soup is the most important of the soup making processes; in fact, these two things soup and stock may be regarded, in many instances, as one and the same. It is important to keep in mind that whenever reference is made to the making of soup usually stock making is also involved and meant. Before the actual soup making processes are taken up, the nature of the ingredients required should be well understood; for this reason, suitable meats and vegetables, which are the principal ingredients in soups, are first discussed.

MEAT USED FOR SOUP MAKING

Almost every kind of meat including beef, veal, mutton, lamb, game and poultry, is used for soup making. When soup stock is made from these meats, they may be cooked separately or as a combination, several kinds may be combined. For instance, mutton used alone makes a very strongly flavored soup, so that it is usually advisable to combine this kind of meat with another meat that has a less distinctive flavor. On the other hand, veal alone does not have sufficient flavor, so it must be combined with lamb, game, fowl or some other well-flavored meat.

Certain cuts of meats are preferred to others in the making of soups because of the difference in their texture. The tender cuts which are the expensive ones, should not be used for soups, as they do not produce enough flavor. The tough cuts, which come from the muscles that the animal uses constantly and that therefore grow hard and tough, are usually cheaper, but they are more suitable because they contain the material that makes the best soup. The pieces best adapted to soup making are the shins, the shanks, the lower part of the round, the neck, the flank, the shoulder, the tail and the brisket. Stock made from one of these cuts will be improved if a small amount of the fat of the meat is cooked with it; but to avoid soup that is too greasy, any excess fat that remains after cooking should be carefully removed. The marrow of the shinbone is the best fat for soup making.

If soup is to be made from fish, a white variety should be selected. The head and trimmings may be utilized, but these alone are not sufficient because soup requires some solid pieces of meat. The same is true of meat bones; they are valuable only when they are used with meat, an equal proportion of bone and meat being required for the best stock.

Soup should always be made entirely of fresh meat that has not been previously cooked. An exception to this rule may sometimes be made in favor of the remains of a piece of roast beef that has been very much under-done in roasting. This may be added to a good piece of raw meat.

Soup made of cold meat has always a vapid, disagreeable taste, very perceptible through all the seasoning and which nothing indeed can disguise. Also, it will be of a bad, dingy color. The juices of the meat having been exhausted by the first cooking, the undue proportion of watery liquid renders it indigestible and unwholesome, as well as unpalatable. As there is little or no nutriment to be derived from soup made with cold meat, it is better to refrain from using it for this purpose and to devote the leavings of the table to some other object. No person accustomed to really good soup, made from fresh meat, can ever be deceived in the taste, even when flavored with wine and spices.

Soup that has been originally made of raw meat entirely is frequently better the second day than the first; provided that it is re-boiled only for a very short time and that no additional water is added to it.

Unless it has been allowed to boil too hard, so as to exhaust the water, the soup-pot will not require replenishing. When it is found absolutely necessary to do so, the additional water must be boiling hot when poured in; if lukewarm or cold, it will entirely spoil the soup.

Every particle of fat should be carefully skimmed from the surface. Greasy soup is disgusting and unwholesome. The lean of meat is much better for soup than the fat.

Long and slow boiling is necessary to extract the strength from the meat. If boiled fast over a large fire, the meat becomes hard and tough and will not give out its juices.

HERBS AND VEGETABLES USED FOR SOUP MAKING

In soup making, a large number of vegetables is used. Any vegetable that has a decided flavor may be used. Among those from which soups can be made successfully are cabbage, cauliflower, asparagus, corn, onions, turnips, carrots, parsnips, tomatoes, beans, peas, lentils, salsify, potatoes, spinach, celery, mushrooms, okra and even sweet potatoes. These vegetables are used to provide flavoring and to form part of the soup itself. When they are used simply for flavoring, they are cooked until their flavor is obtained and then removed from the stock. When they are to form part of the soup, as well as to impart flavor, they are left in the soup in small pieces or made into a puree and eaten with the soup.

The cook should season the soup but very slightly with salt and pepper. If he puts in too much, it may spoil it for the taste of most of those that are to eat it; but if too little, it is easy to add more to your own plate.

The herbs usually used in soups are parsley, common thyme, summer savory, knotted marjoram, and other seasonings such as bay leaves, tarragon, allspice, cinnamon, nutmeg, cloves, nutmeg, black and white pepper, red pepper etc.

Attention must be given to the condition of the vegetables that are used in soup. The fresh vegetables that are used should be in perfect condition. They should have no decayed places that might taint or discolor the soups and they should be as crisp and solid as possible. When dried vegetables are to be used for soup making, they should first be soaked well in cold water and then, before being added to the stock, either partly cooked or entirely cooked and made into a puree.

PROCESSES INVOLVED IN MAKING STOCK

Although the making of stock or soup is a simple process, it must necessarily be a rather long one. The reason for this is that all flavors cannot be drawn from the soup materials unless they are subjected to long, slow cooking at a temperature lower than the boiling point. With this point definitely understood, the actual work of soup making may be taken up.

COOKING MEAT FOR SOUP

When clear stock is to be made from fresh meat, the required quantity of meat should be cut into small pieces so as to expose as much of the surface as possible from which the flavor of the meat can be drawn. A little more flavor is obtained and a brown color developed if a small part, perhaps a fourth, of the pieces of meat is first browned in the frying pan. The pieces thus browned, together with the pieces of fresh meat, are put into a kettle and a quart of cold water for each pound of meat is then added.

The reason for using cold rather than hot water will be evident when the action of water on raw meat is understood. The fiber of meat is composed of innumerable thread-like tubes containing the flavor that is to be drawn out into the water in order to make the stock appetizing.

When the meat is cut, these tiny tubes are laid open. Putting the meat thus prepared into cold water and allowing it to heat gradually tend to extract the contents of the tubes. This material is known as extractives and it contains in its composition stimulating substances. On the other hand, plunging the meat into hot water and subjecting it quickly to a high temperature will coagulate the protein in the tissue and prevent the extractives from leaving the tubes.

To obtain the most flavors from meat that is properly prepared, it should be put over a slow fire and allowed to come gradually to the boiling point. As the water approaches the boiling point, a scum consisting of coagulated albumin, blood, and foreign material will begin to rise to the top. This should be skimmed off at once and the process of skimming must be continued until no scum remains. When the water begins to boil rapidly, the fire should be lowered so that the water will bubble only enough for a very slight motion to be observed. Throughout the cooking, the meat should not be allowed to boil violently or to cease bubbling entirely.

The meat should be allowed to cook for at least 4 hours, but longer if possible. If, during this long cooking, too much water evaporates, more should be added to dilute the stock. The salt that is required for seasoning may be added just a few minutes before the stock is removed from the kettle. However, it is better to add the salt together with the other seasonings after the stock has been drawn off, for salt, has a tendency to harden the tissues of meat and to prevent the flavor from being readily extracted.

Although, as has been explained, flavor is drawn from the fibers of meat by boiling it slowly for a long time, the cooking of meat for soup does not extract the nourishment from it to any extent. In reality, the meat itself largely retains its original nutritive value after it has been cooked for soup, although a small quantity of protein is drawn out and much of the fat is removed. This meat should never be wasted; rather, it should be used carefully with materials that will take the place of the flavor that has been cooked from it.

REMOVING GREASE FROM SOUP

A greasy soup is always unpalatable. Therefore, a very important feature of soup making, whether a thin or a thick soup is being made, is the removal of all grease. Various ways of removing grease have been devised depending on whether the soup is hot or cold. In the case of hot or warm soup, all the grease that it is possible to remove with a spoon may be skimmed from the top and the remainder then taken up with a piece of clean blotting paper, tissue-paper or absorbent cotton. Another plan by which the fat may be hardened and then collected, consists in tying a few small pieces of ice in a piece of cloth and drawing them over the surface of the soup. A very simple method is to allow the soup or stock to become cold, and then remove the fat, which collects on the top and hardens, by merely lifting off the cake that forms.

CLEARING SOUP

Sometimes it is desired to improve the appearance of soup stock particularly a small amount of soup that is to be served at a very dainty luncheon or dinner. In order to do this, the stock may be treated by a certain process that will cause it to become clear. After being cleared, it may be served as a thin soup or, if it is heavy enough, it may be made into a clear, sparkling jelly into which many desirable things may be molded for salad or for a dish to accompany a heavy course. Clearing soup is rather extravagant; however, while it does not improve the taste, it does improve the appearance.

A very satisfactory way in which to clear stock is to use egg whites and crushed eggshell. To each quart of cold stock should be added the crushed shell and a slightly beaten egg white. These should be mixed well, placed on the fire, and the mixture stirred constantly until it boils.

As the egg coagulates, some of the floating particles in the stock are caught and carried to the top while others are carried to the bottom by the particles of shell as they settle. After the mixture has boiled for 5 or 10 minutes, the top should be skimmed carefully and the stock then strained through a fine cloth.

When it has been reheated, the cleared stock will be ready to serve.

THICKENING SOUP

Although thin, clear soups are preferred by some and are particularly desirable for their stimulating effect, thick soups find much favor when they are used to form a substantial part of a meal. Besides giving consistency to soup, thickening usually improves the flavor but its chief purpose is to give nutritive value to this food. In fact, whenever a soup is thickened, its food value is increased by the ingredient thus added. For this reason, it is advisable to thicken soups when they are desired for any other purpose than their stimulating effect.

The substance used to thicken soups may be either a starchy material or food or a puree of some food. The starchy materials generally used for this purpose are plain flour, browned flour, corn starch and arrowroot flour. Any one of these should be moistened with enough cold water to make a mixture that will pour easily and then added to the hot liquid while the soup is stirred constantly to prevent the formation of lumps.

A sufficient amount of this thickening material should be used to make a soup of the consistency of heavy cream.

The starchy foods that are used for thickening include rice, barley, oatmeal, noodles, tapioca, sago and macaroni. Many unusual and fancy forms of macaroni can be secured or the plain varieties of Italian pastes may be broken into small pieces and cooked with the soup. When any of these foods are used, they should be added long enough before the soup is removed to be cooked thoroughly.

Purees of beans, peas, lentils, potatoes and other vegetables are especially desirable for the thickening of soups, for they not only give consistency, but add nutritive value and flavor as well. Another excellent thickening may be obtained by beating raw eggs and then adding them carefully to the soup just before it is to be served. After eggs have been added for thickening, the soup should not be allowed to boil, as it is liable to curdle.

SERVING SOUP

Soup may be correctly served in several different ways, the method to adopt usually depending on the kind of soup. The spoon to be served with soup also depends on the kind of soup, but a larger spoon than a teaspoon is always necessary. When soup is served in a soup plate, a dessertspoon is used. Bouillon spoon is the best kind to use with any thin soup served in bouillon cups. Such a spoon is about the length of a Teaspoon, but has a round bowl.

To increase the attractiveness of soup and at the same time make it more appetizing and nutritious, various accompaniments and relishes are served with it. Many soups, especially vegetable soups, are improved in flavor by the addition of a spoonful of grated cheese, which should be sprinkled into the dish at the time of serving.

In summer clear soups are sometimes served cold, as cold soups are found more desirable for warm weather than hot ones. However, when a soup is intended to be hot, it should be hot when it is ready to be eaten and every effort should be made to have it in this condition if an appetizing soup is desired. This can be accomplished if the soup is thoroughly heated before it is removed from the stove and the dishes in which it is to be served are warmed before the soup is put into them.

RECIPES – STOCKS

WHITE STOCK

Ingredients: 5 lb. veal, 1 fowl, 3 or 4 lb., 8 qt. cold water, 2 medium-sized onions, 2 Tb. butter, 2 stalks celery, 1 blade nutmeg, Salt and Pepper as necessary.

Cut the veal and fowl into pieces and add the cold water. Place on a slow fire, and let come gradually to the boiling point. Skim carefully and place where it will simmer gently for 6 hours. Slice the onions, brown slightly in the butter, and add to the stock with the celery and nutmeg.

Salt and pepper to suit taste. Cook 1 hour longer and then strain and cool. Remove the fat before using.

BROWN SOUP STOCK

Ingredients: 6 lbs. shin of beef, 3 to 6 quarts cold water, 1 bay leaf, 6 cloves, 1 tablespoon mixed herbs, 2 sprigs parsley, 1/2 cup carrot, 1/2 cup turnip, 1/2 cup celery and 1/2 cup onion.

Wipe beef and cut lean meat into cubes; brown one-third in hot frying pan; put remaining two-thirds with bone and fat into soup kettle; add water and let stand 30 minutes. Place on back of range; add browned meat and heat gradually to boiling point. Cover and cook slowly four hours; add vegetables and seasoning one hour before it is finished. Strain and put away to cool. Remove all fat; reheat and serve.

VEGETABLE STOCK.

To 4 qts. water allow 1 pint lentils, or rather less than 1 pint haricots. In addition allow 1 carrot, 1 turnip, 1 onion, and 1/4 head of celery. Clean apple peelings and cores, and any fresh vegetable cuttings may also be added with advantage. For white stock, use the white haricot beans, rice, or macaroni in place of lentils or brown haricots. Soak the pulse Overnight, and simmer with the vegetables for 4 hours. Any stock not used should be emptied out of the stockpot, and boiled up afresh each day.

FISH STOCK -1

Place a saucepan over the fire with a good-sized piece of sweet butter and a sliced onion; put into that some sliced tomatoes, then add as many different kinds of fish as you can get oysters, clams, smelts, pawns, crabs, shrimps and all kinds of pan-fish; cook all together until the onions are well browned; then add a bunch of sweet herbs, salt and pepper, and sufficient water to make the required amount of stock. After this has cooked for half an hour pound it with a wooden pestle, then strain and cook again until it jellies.

FISH STOCK -2

Fish for nearly all dishes is better if boned before cooking; it is also economy to do this, as the bones can then be used for stock for fish soups.

These soups, although not well known here at present, are a valuable food; they are easy to make, wholesome, and nourishing. After the fillets of fish have been removed, directions for which are given amongst the fish recipes, take the bones, wash them well in cold water, and cut away any black substance that may be adhering to them. Break them up and put into a saucepan with a teaspoonful of salt; when it boils remove the scum and put in one dozen white peppercorns, a fagot of herbs, one onion, and one carrot; boil steadily for two hours or longer, strain through a sieve into a basin, and it is ready for use.

STOCK FROM BONES -1

Beef bones are the best for this stock; break them up very small with a chopper, put them into a large saucepan and cover well with cold water, add two teaspoonfuls of salt, and when it boils up remove the scum carefully, and put in one onion, one carrot, half a turnip, a little piece of the outside stalk of celery, and one dozen peppercorns. Boil steadily for six hours, or longer, then strain off through a colander or sieve, and stand in a cool place till the next day. Carefully remove the fat by directions given elsewhere, and it is ready for use. This stock is a good foundation for all soups, gravies, and sauces.

STOCK FROM BONES -2

The bones from all joints of meat, whether roasted or boiled, make excellent stock. Beef bones are the best, but very good stock can be made from mutton and veal bones. The bones and trimmings of all kinds of poultry, game, and rabbits are also excellent, particularly for soups that require a special flavor. To make this stock successfully care must be taken to remove all pieces that may be burnt, as these give the stock an unpleasant flavor. The bones must be chopped very small, and well covered with cold water. When the pot boils put in a teaspoonful of salt and skim well, then boil steadily for six hours or longer; strain off and remove the fat, and it is ready for use, but it is much better to let it stand till the next day before converting it into soup or gravy.

VEAL STOCK

The butcher should chop the bones very small. Cut the meat across in several places, lay it in a very clean stock pot, cover well with cold water, and bring to the boil slowly; put in a dessertspoonful of salt, and skim very carefully; draw away from the fire, place it where it will boil steadily, put in 2 dozen white peppercorns, one onion stuck with six cloves, and a fagot of herbs. This is made with a sprig each of parsley, marjoram, and thyme, tied up with a bay or peach leaf; boil steadily for six hours, and strain off. This is the foundation for the best white soups and sauces; it is also a very nutritious broth for invalids. The meat can be made hot again in about half a pint of the stock and served with parsley butter sauce.

BEEF STOCK -1

Take Leg of Beef, the bone in this meat should be chopped small. Remove the marrow from the bones, and cut the meat into small pieces; put all together into a stock pot or digester, cover well with cold water, and bring it to the boil; add a dessertspoonful of salt; this will throw up the scum, which must be carefully removed. When this has been done put in 2 dozen peppercorns, an onion, and two carrots, draw away from the fire and let it boil steadily for five or six hours or longer, then strain off through a colander and stand away in a cool place. This is the foundation for nearly all-good brown soups. The bones boiled again will make second stock, and the meat does very well for brawn, a recipe for which is given amongst the meat dishes.

BEEF STOCK -2

Ingredients: 1 pound of round of beef, 2 quarts of water, 2 small, new carrots, or 1/2 of a carrot, 1/2 pound of beef bones, 2 small potatoes, 1 onion, 1 tomato, fresh or canned Parsley.

Boil the beef, bones, and vegetables in two quarts of water over a slow fire adding pepper and salt. Skim occasionally, and after two hours add two tablespoons of sherry; then strain through fine soup-strainer or cheesecloth. This is the basis of all the following soups, except when otherwise stated. To make this stock richer, add a turkey leg to above receipt; boil one and a half hours, then add one-half a pound of finely chopped beef. Cook for half an hour longer, then strain.

SCOTCH MUTTON BROTH

Six pounds neck of mutton, three quarts water, five carrots, five turnips, two onions, four tablespoonfuls barley, a little salt. Soak mutton in water for an hour, cut off scrag, and put it in stew pan with three quarts of water. As soon as it boils, skim well, and then simmer for one and one-half hours. Cut best end of mutton into cutlets, dividing it with two bones in each; take off nearly all fat before you put it into broth; skim the moment the meat boils, and every ten minutes afterwards; add carrots, turnips and onions, all cut into two or three pieces, then put them into soup soon enough to be thoroughly done; stir in barley; add salt to taste; let all stew together for three and one-half hours; about one-half hour before sending it to table, put in little chopped parsley and serve. You may thicken the soup with rice or barley that has first been soaked in cold water, or with green peas, or with young corn, cut down from the cob, or with tomatoes, scalded, peeled and cut into pieces.

SCOTCH BROTH

Soak over night two tablespoonfuls of pearl barley and one of coarse oatmeal, in water sufficient to cover them. In the morning, put the grains, together with the water in which they were soaked, into two quarts of water and simmer for several hours, adding boiling water as needed. About an hour before the soup is required, add a turnip cut into small dice, a grated carrot, and one half cup of fine pieces of the brown portion of the crust of a loaf of whole-wheat bread. Rub all through a colander, and add salt, a cup of milk, and a half-cup of thin cream. This should make about three pints of soup.

CREAM SOUP STOCK

This is the foundation or sauce for many fish and vegetable cream soups.

1 quart milk
1 teaspoon salt
1 teaspoon white pepper
2 tablespoons flour
1 tablespoon butter
1 cup boiling water

Scald milk and add seasoning; thicken with flour and butter rubbed to a cream with boiling water and boil two minutes.

For potato soup use 6 large or 10 medium-sized potatoes boiled and mashed fine. Stir into milk, proceed as above, and strain. Add tablespoon chopped parsley just before serving.

For pea soup boil and mash 2 cups green peas and add to sauce.

For cream of celery boil 2 cups cut celery until tender; rub through sieve, add to milk and proceed as above.

For corn soup use same foundation, adding a can of corn, or corn cut from 6 ears boiled fresh corn and boil 15 minutes.

For cream of fish soup add to milk about one pound of boiled fish, rubbed through sieve and proceed as above.

BRAN STOCK

For every quart of stock desired, boil a cup of good wheat bran in three pints of water for two or three hours or until reduced one third. This stock may be made the base of a variety of palatable and nutritious soups by flavoring with different vegetables and seasoning with salt and cream. An excellent soup may be prepared by flavoring the stock with celery, or by the addition of a quantity of strained stewed tomato sufficient to disguise the taste of the stock. It is also valuable in giving consistence to soups, in the preparation of some of which it may be advantageously used in place of other liquid.

BARLEY BROTH

1 carrot, 1 turnip, 4 leeks or 3 small onions, 4 sprigs parsley, 4 sticks celery, 1 tea-cup pearl barley, 3 qts. Water. (The celery may be omitted if desired, or, when in season, 1 teacup green peas may be substituted).

Scrub clean (but do not peel) the carrot and turnip. Wash celery, parsley, and barley. Shred all the vegetables finely; put in saucepan with the water. Bring to the boil and slowly simmer for 2 to 3 hours. Add the chopped parsley and serve.

STOCK FOR CLEAR SOUP OR BOUILLON

Ingredients: 4 lb. beef, 4 qt. cold water, 1 medium-sized onion, 1 stalk celery, 2 sprigs parsley, 6 whole cloves, 12 peppercorns, 1 bay leaf, Salt and Pepper as necessary.

Cut the meat into small pieces. Pour the cold water over it, place on a slow fire, and let it come to a boil. Skim off all scum that rises to the top. Cover tightly and keep at the simmering point for 6 to 8 hours. Then strain and remove the fat. Add the onion and celery cut into pieces, the parsley, cloves, peppercorns, and bay leaf. Simmer gently for about 20 minutes. Add salt and pepper to taste. Strain through a cloth.

CONSOMME

One of the most delicious of the thin, clear broths is consomme. This is usually served plain, but any material that will not cloud it, such as finely diced vegetables, green peas, tiny pieces of fowl or meat, may, if desired, be added to it before it is served. As a rule, only a very small quantity of such material is used for each serving.

Ingredients: 4 lb. lower round of beef, 4 lb. shin of veal, 1/4 c. butter, 8 qt. cold water, 1 small carrot, 1 large onion, 2 stalks celery, 12 peppercorns, 5 cloves, 4 sprigs parsley, Pinch summer savory, Pinch thyme, 2 bay leaves, Salt and Pepper as necessary.

Cut the beef and veal into small pieces. Put the butter and meat into the stock kettle, and stir over the fire until the meat begins to brown.

Add the cold water, and let come to the boiling point. Skim carefully and let simmer for 6 hours. Cut the vegetables into small pieces and add to the stock with the spices and herbs. Cook for 1 hour, adding salt and pepper to suit taste. Strain and cool. Remove the fat and clear according to directions previously given.

RECIPES - SOUPS

ASPARAGUS SOUP

Wash two bunches of fresh asparagus carefully, and cut into small pieces. Put to cook in a quart of boiling water, and simmer gently till perfectly tender, when there should remain about a pint of the liquor. Turn into a colander, and rub all through except the hard portion. To a pint of asparagus mixture add salt and one cup of thin cream and a pint of milk; boil up for a few minutes, and serve.

1/2 dozen sticks of asparagus, 1/2-pint water, 1/4-pint milk, 1 level dessertspoonful of corn flour, 1/4 oz. of butter, pepper and salt to taste. Boil the asparagus in the water till tender, add the seasoning, and the corn flour smoothed in the milk, boil up and serve.

ASPARAGUS CREAM

For making two quarts of soup, use two bundles of fresh asparagus. Cut the tops from one of the bunches and cook them twenty minutes in salted water, enough to cover them. Cook the remainder of the asparagus about twenty minutes in a quart of stock or water. Cut an onion into thin slices and fry in three tablespoonfuls of butter ten minutes, being careful not to scorch it; then add the asparagus that has been boiled in the stock; cook this five minutes, stirring constantly; then add three tablespoonfuls of dissolved flour, cook five minutes longer. Turn this mixture into the boiling stock and boil twenty minutes. Rub through a sieve; add the milk and cream and the asparagus heads. If water is used in place of stock, use all cream.

APPLE SOUP -1

1 lb. apples, 1 qt. water, sugar and flavouring, 1 tablespoon sago.

Wash the apples and cut into quarters, but do not peel or core. Put into a saucepan with the water and sugar and flavoring to taste. When sweet, ripe apples can be obtained, people with natural tastes will prefer no addition of any kind. Otherwise, a little cinnamon, cloves, or the yellow part of lemon rind may be added. Stew until the apples are soft. Strain through a sieve, rubbing the apple pulp through, but leaving cores, etc., behind. Wash the sago, add to the strained soup, and boil gently for 1 hour. Stir now and then, as the sago is apt to stick to the pan.

1 large cooking apple, 1 small finely chopped onion, seasoning and sugar to taste, a little butter, 1 teaspoonful of cornflour, 1/2 pint of water.

Peel and cut up the apple, and cook with the onion in the water till quite tender. Rub the mixture through a sieve, return to the saucepan, add the butter, seasoning and sugar, thicken the soup with the cornflour, and serve.

ARTICHOKE SOUP

1 lb. each of artichokes and potatoes, 1 Spanish onion, 1 oz. of butter, 1 pint of milk, and pepper and salt to taste. Peel, wash, and cut into dice the artichokes, potatoes, and onion. Cook them until tender in 1 quart of water with the butter and seasoning. When the vegetables are tender rub them through a sieve. Return the liquid to the saucepan, add the milk, and boil the soup up again. Add water if the soup is too thick. Serve with Allinson plain rusks, or small dice of bread fried crisp in butter or vege-butter.

BEEF SOUP

Select a small shin of beef of moderate size, crack the bone in small pieces, wash and place it in a kettle to boil, with five or six quarts of cold water. Let it boil about two hours, or until it begins to get tender, then season it with a tablespoonful of salt, and a teaspoonful of pepper; boil it one hour longer, then add to it one carrot, two turnips, two tablespoonfuls of rice or pearl barley, one head of celery, and a teaspoonful of summer savory powdered fine; the vegetables to be minced up in small pieces like dice. After these ingredients have boiled a quarter of an hour, put in two potatoes cut up in small pieces, let it boil half an hour longer; take the meat from the soup, and if intended to be served with it, take out the bones and lay it closely and neatly on a dish, and garnish with sprigs of parsley. Serve made mustard and catsup with it. It is very nice pressed and eaten cold with mustard and vinegar, or catsup. Four hours are required for making this soup. Should any remain over the first day, it may be heated, with the addition of a little boiling water, and served again. Some fancy a glass of brown sherry added just before being served. Serve very hot.

BEAN SOUP

2 cups beans
2 tablespoons finely cut onion
2 tablespoons finely cut bacon
1 teaspoon salt
1/8 teaspoon pepper
2 tablespoons chopped parsley
1 teaspoon thyme
3 tablespoons flour

Soak beans in water over night. Drain and put into saucepan with six cups boiling water and boil slowly two hours or until soft; add onion and bacon which have been fried light brown; boil five minutes; add salt, pepper, parsley and thyme. Mash beans with back of spoon. Add flour which has been mixed with a little cold water; boil five minutes and serve.

BAKED BEAN SOUP

Soak a half pint of white beans over night. In the morning turn off the water, and place them in an earthen dish with two or two and one half quarts of boiling water; cover and let them simmer in a moderate oven four or five hours. Also soak over night a tablespoonful of pearl tapioca in sufficient water to cover. When the beans are soft, rub through a colander, after which add the soaked tapioca, and salt if desired; also as much powdered thyme as can be taken on the point of a penknife and sufficient water to make the soup of proper consistency if the water has mostly evaporated. Return to the oven, and cook one half hour longer. A little cream may be added just before serving.

BEAN AND CORN SOUP

Cold boiled or stewed corn and cold baked beans form the basis of this soup. Take one pint of each, rub through a colander, add a slice of onion, three cups of boiling water or milk, and boil for ten minutes. Turn through the colander a second time to remove the onion and any lumps or skins which may remain. Season with salt and a half cup of cream. If preferred, the onion may be omitted.

BEAN AND HOMINY SOUP

Soak separately in cold water over night a cupful each of dry beans and hominy. In the morning, boil them together till both are perfectly tender and broken to pieces. Rub through a colander, and add sufficient milk to make three pints. Season with salt, and stir in a cup of whipped cream just before serving. Cold beans and hominy may be utilized for this soup.

BEAN AND POTATO SOUP

Soak a half pint of dry white beans over night; in the morning drain and put to cook in boiling water. When tender, rub through a colander.

Prepare sliced potato sufficient to make one quart, cook in as small a quantity of water as possible, rub through a colander, and add to the beans. Add milk or water sufficient to make two quarts, and as much prepared thyme as can be taken on the point of a penknife, with salt to season. Boil for a few minutes, add a teacup of thin cream, and serve.

BEAN AND TOMATO SOUP

Take one pint of boiled or a little less of mashed beans, one pint of stewed tomatoes, and rub together through a colander. Add salt, a cup of thin cream, one half a cup of nicely steamed rice, and sufficient boiling water to make a soup of the proper consistency. Reheat and serve.

BISQUE SOUP

Have ready a good broth made of three pounds of veal boiled slowly in as much water as will cover it, till the meat is reduced to shreds. It must then be well strained.

Having boiled one fine middle-sized lobster, extract all the meat from the body and claws. Bruise part of the coral in a mortar, and also an equal quantity of the meat. Mix them well together. Add nutmeg, cayenne, salt and pepper, and make them up into force meat balls, binding the mixture with the yolk of an egg slightly beaten. Take three quarts of the veal broth and put it into the meat of the lobster cut into mouthfuls. Boil it together about twenty minutes.

Then thicken it with the remaining coral (which you must first rub through a sieve), and add the force meat balls and a little butter rolled in flour. Simmer it gently for ten minutes, but do not let it come to a boil, as that will injure the color. Serve with small dice of bread fried brown in butter.

BLACK BEAN SOUP

Soak a pint (0.5 quart) of black beans over night in cold water. When ready to cook, put into two and one half quarts of fresh water, which should be boiling, and simmer until completely dissolved, adding more boiling water from time to time if needed. There should be about two quarts of all when done. Rub through a colander, add salt, a half cup of cream, and reheat. When hot, turn through a soup strainer, add two or more teaspoonfuls of lemon juice, and serve.

A pint of black beans, soaked over night in three quarts of water. In the morning pour off this water, and add three quarts of fresh. Boil gently six hours. When done, there should be one quart. Add a quart of stock, six whole cloves, six whole allspice, a small piece of nutmeg, a small piece of cinnamon, stalk of celery, a bouquet of sweet herbs, also one good-sized onion and one small slice each of turnip and carrot, all cut fine and fried in three table-spoonfuls of butter. Into the butter remaining in the pan put a spoonful of flour, and cook until brown. Add to soup, and simmer all together one hour. Season with salt and pepper, and rub through a fine sieve. Serve with slices of lemon and egg balls, the lemon to be put in the tureen with the soup.

BROWN SOUP

Take six pounds of the lean of fresh beef, cut from the bone. Stick it over with four dozen cloves. Season it with a tea-spoonful of salt, a teaspoonful of pepper, a tea-spoonful of nutmeg, and a beaten nutmeg. Slice half a dozen onions; fry them in butter; chop them, and spread them over the meat after you have put it into the soup-pot. Pour in five quarts of water, and stew it slowly for five or six hours; skimming it well.

When the meat has dissolved into shreds, strain it, and return the liquid to the pot. Then add a tumbler and a half, or six wine glasses of claret or port wine. Simmer it again slowly till dinner time. When the soup is reduced to three quarts, it is done enough. Put it into a tureen, and send it to table.

Simmer together two pints of sliced potatoes and one third as much of the thin brown shavings (not thicker than a silver dime) from the top of a loaf of whole-wheat bread, in one quart of water. The crust must not be burned or blackened, and must not include any of the soft portion of the loaf. When the potatoes are tender, mash all through a colander. Flavor with a cup of strained, stewed tomatoes, a little salt, and return to the fire; when hot, add a half cup of cream, and boiling water to make the soup of proper consistency, and serve at once. If care has been taken to prepare the crust as directed, this soup will have a brown color and a fine, pungent flavor exceedingly pleasant to the taste.

BROWN MACARONI SOUP

Take 1 1/2 oz. Macaroni, 1 oz. Butter, Vegetables, Corn flour and 2 quarts Bone Stock. Slice up the onions or leeks, one carrot, and make a fagot of herbs; fry them in the butter with 1 dozen peppercorns till they are quite brown, but not burnt. Sprinkle over a tablespoonful of corn flour, and when brown pour over the boiling stock and stir till it boils up; let it simmer for an hour. If it is not brown enough, burn a little sugar in a spoon and stir it in. If half a teaspoonful of sugar is sprinkled over the vegetables when they are frying they will brown much quicker. When the vegetables are soft rub the soup through a wire sieve and return to the saucepan. Boil the macaroni in salt and water for twenty minutes, strain off, and cut into pieces one inch long; put these into the soup and simmer for a quarter of an hour. Flavor with a little salt and pepper if necessary, and pour into a hot tureen.

BARLEY SOUP

8 oz. of pearl barley, 2 onions, 4 potatoes, 1/2 a teaspoonful of thyme, 1 dessertspoonful of finely chopped parsley, 3-1/2 pints of water, 1/2 pint of milk, 1 oz. of butter. Pick and wash the barley, chop up the onions, slice the potatoes. Boil the whole gently for 4 hours with the water, adding the butter, thyme, pepper and salt to taste. When the barley is quite soft, add the milk and parsley, boil the soup up, and serve.

BREAD SOUP

1/2 lb. of stale crusts of Allinson wholemeal bread, 4 onions, 2 turnips, 1 stick of celery, 1 oz. of butter, 1/2 oz. of finely chopped parsley, 8 pints of water, 1/2 pint of milk. Soak the crusts in the water for 2 hours before they are put over the fire. Cut up into small dice the vegetables; add them to the bread with the butter and pepper and salt to taste. Allow all to simmer gently for 1 hour, then rub the soup through a sieve, return it to the saucepan, add the milk and parsley, and, if the flavor is liked, a little grated nutmeg; boil the soup up and serve at once.

1 slice of bread, 1 small finely chopped onion fried brown, a pinch of nutmeg, pepper and salt to taste. Boil the bread in 3/4 pint of water and milk in equal parts, adding the onion and seasoning. When the bread is quite tender, rub all through a sieve, return soup to the saucepan, boil up, and serve.

BUTTER BEAN SOUP

2 oz. of butter beans soaked overnight in 1 pint of water, 1/2 small onion cut up small, 2 oz. carrot, 2 oz. celery, 1/2 oz. butter. Cook all the vegetables until tender, adding water as it boils away. When all is tender, rub the vegetables through a sieve, return to the saucepan, season with pepper and salt, add the butter, boil up the soup, and serve.

CABBAGE SOUP

1 fair-sized cabbage, a large Spanish onion, 1-1/2 oz. of butter, pepper and salt to taste, 1/2 salt spoonful of nutmeg, 1-1/2 pints of milk, 2 tablespoonfuls of Allinson fine wheat meal. After preparing and washing the cabbage, shred up very fine, chop up the onion, set these two in a saucepan over the fire with 1 quart of water, the butter and seasoning, and let all cook gently for 1 hour, or longer it the vegetables are not quite tender. Add the milk and thickening when the vegetables are thoroughly tender, and let all simmer gently for 10 minutes; serve with little squares of toasted or fried bread, or Allinson plain rusks.

Take 1 Cabbage, 2 oz. Butter, 1 pint Milk, Pepper, Salt, and Bread. Wash and strain the cabbage well, and cut it up into slices; throw it into boiling salt and water, and cook for five minutes; strain all the water off and put it into a saucepan with the salt, pepper, and two quarts of boiling water, and boil for one hour. Add the milk and let it boil up again, toast the slice of bread and cut it up into dice. Put it into a warm soup tureen and pour the boiling soup over it.

CABBAGE AND BACON SOUP

Tale 1 Cabbage, 1 lb. Bacon, 1 doz. Peppercorns, 2 Turnips, 1 Carrot, 1 Onion and Pieces of Stale Bread. This soup is not as expensive as it appears, for the bacon is served as a dish of meat, either after the soup or cold for breakfast or tea. Put two quarts of water into a saucepan; when it boils put in a pound of bacon neither too lean nor too fat. Let it boil slowly for one hour. The bacon must be well washed and scraped before cooking, and when it boils skim the pot thoroughly. Well wash the cabbage and soak it in hot water for half an hour. Take all the water away and put the cabbage into the saucepan with the bacon and vegetables cut up, and the peppercorns tied in a piece of muslin; let them simmer together for two and a half hours, take up the cabbage, and cut it into quarters. Take one quarter and cut it into small pieces and put it into a soup tureen. Cut some stale pieces of bread into thin slices and lay on the top, pour over the boiling liquor, and serve. Dish the bacon, pull off the rind, and put the rest of the cabbage round the dish.

CAPER SOUP

2 pints of water, 1 pint of milk, 1 large tablespoonful of capers, 1/2 lemon, 2 eggs, 1-1/2 oz. of Allinson fine wheatmeal, 1/2 oz. of butter, pepper and salt to taste. Boil the milk and water and butter, with seasoning to taste; thicken it with the wheatmeal rubbed smooth with a little milk.

Chop up the capers, add them and let the soup cook gently for 10 minutes; take it off the fire, beat up the eggs and add them carefully, that they may not curdle; at the last add the juice of the half lemon, re-heat the soup without allowing it to boil, and serve.

CARROT SOUP

4 good-sized carrots, 1 small head of celery, 1 fair-sized onion, 1 turnip, 3 oz. of breadcrumbs, 1-1/2 oz. of butter, 1 blade of nutmeg, pepper and salt to taste. Scrape and wash the vegetables, and cut them up small; set them over the fire with 3 pints of water, the butter, bread, and nutmeg. Let all boil together, until the vegetables are quite tender, and then rub them through a sieve. Return the mixture to the saucepan, season with pepper and salt, and if too thick add water to the soup, which should be as thick as cream, boil the soup up, and serve.

For a quart of soup, slice one large carrot and boil in a small quantity of water for two hours or longer, then rub it through a colander, add a quart of rich milk, and salt to season.

Reheat, and when boiling, thicken with two teaspoonfuls of flour rubbed smooth in a little cold milk.

CALF'S HEAD SOUP

Scald and clean the head, and put it to boil with two gallons of water, a shank of veal, three onions, two carrots, a little bacon, and a bunch of sweet herbs. When they have boiled half an hour, take out the head and shank of veal, and cut all the meat off the bones into pieces of two inches square; let the soup boil half an hour longer, when strain it, and put in the meat; season it with salt, cayenne and black pepper, and cloves, if you like; thicken it with butter and browned flour, and let it boil nearly an hour; put some fried force meat balls in the tureen, and just before you pour out the soup, stir into it a table-spoonful of sugar, browned in a frying pan, and half a pint of wine. This resembles turtle soup.

CAULIFLOWER SOUP

1 medium-sized cauliflower, 1-1/2 pints of milk, 1 oz. of butter, 2 oz. of Allinson fine wheatmeal, pepper and salt to taste, a little nutmeg, and the juice of a lemon. Prepare the cauliflower by washing and breaking it into pieces, keeping the flowers whole, and boil in 1-1/2 pints of water, adding the butter, nutmeg, and seasoning. When the cauliflower is quite tender add the milk, boil it up, and thicken the soup with the wheatmeal, which should first be smoothed with a little cold water. Lastly, add the lemon juice, and serve the soup with sippets of toast.

CATFISH SOUP

The small white catfishes are the best. Having cut off their heads, skins the fish, and cleans them, and cut them in three. To twelve small catfish allow a pound and a half of chicken. Cut the chicken into small pieces, or slice it very thin, and scald it two or three times in boiling water, lest it be too salt. Chop together a bunch of parsley and some sweet marjoram stripped from the stalks. Put these ingredients into a soup kettle and season them with pepper: the chicken will make it salt enough. Add a head of celery cut small, or a large table-spoonful of celery seed tied up in a bit of clear muslin to prevent its dispersing. Pat in two quarts of water, cover the kettle, and let it boil slowly till every thing is sufficiently done, and the fish and chicken quite tender. Skim it frequently. Boil in another vessel a quart of rich milk, in which you have melted a quarter of a pound of butter divided into small bits and rolled in flour. Pour it hot to the soup, and stir in at the last the beaten yolks of four eggs. Give it another boil, just to take off the rawness of the eggs, and then put it into a tureen, taking out the bag of celery seed before you send the soup to table, and adding some toasted bread cut into small squares. In making toast for soap, cut the bread thick, and pare off all the crust.

COCOANUT SOUP

2 cocoanuts grated, 2 blades of nutmeg, 1 salt spoonful of cinnamon, 3 pints of water, the juice of a lemon, 2 eggs, 1 oz. of Allinson fine wheatmeal, pepper and salt to taste. Boil the cocoanut in the water, adding the nutmeg, cinnamon, and seasoning. Let it cook gently for an hour; strain the mixture through a sieve and then return the soup to the saucepan. Make a paste of the eggs, wheatmeal, and lemon juice, add it to the soup and let it boil up before serving; let it simmer for 5 minutes, and serve with a little plain boiled rice.

CORN SOUP

1 cup of fresh corn, 1 quart of water, 1/2 pint of milk, 1/2 oz. of butter, 1/2 oz. of finely chopped parsley, 1 oz. of eschalots, seasoning to taste.

Steep the corn over night in the water and boil it in the same water for 3 hours, add the butter, the eschalots, chopped up very fine, and pepper and salt. Let the whole simmer very gently for another 1/2 hour, add the milk and parsley boil the soup up once more, and serve.

CLEAR SOUP

1 large Spanish onion, 1 teaspoonful of mixed herbs, 1/2 head of celery, 1-1/2 oz. butter, 1 carrot, 1 turnip, and pepper and salt to taste. Chop the onion up fine, and fry it brown in the butter, in the saucepan in which the soup is to be made, and add 5 pints of water. Prepare and cut into small pieces the carrot, turnip, and celery; add these, the nutmeg, herbs, and pepper and salt to the water, with the fried onions. When the vegetables are tender drain the liquid; return it to the saucepan, and boil the soup up.

CLEAR SOUP WITH DUMPLINGS

2 large onions, 1 teaspoonful of herbs, 1/2 teaspoonful of nutmeg, 1 carrot, 1 turnip, pepper and salt to taste, 1 oz. of butter, 3 pints of water.

Chop up finely the onions and fry them brown in the butter in the saucepan in which the soup is to be made; add the water. Cut up in thin slices the carrot and turnip, add these, with the herbs, nutmeg, and seasoning to the soup. Let it boil for I hour, drain the liquid, return it to the saucepan, and when boiling add the dumplings prepared as follows: 1/2 pint of clear soup, 4 eggs, a little nutmeg, pepper and salt to taste.

Beat the eggs well, mix them with the soup, and season the mixture with nutmeg, pepper, and salt. Pour it into a buttered jug; set it in a pan with boiling water, and let the mixture thicken. Then cut off little lumps with a spoon, and throw these into the soup and boil up before serving.

CLEAR CELERY SOUP

1 large head of celery or 2 small ones, 1 large Spanish onion, 2 oz. of butter, pepper and salt to taste, and 1 blade of nutmeg. Chop the onion and fry it brown in the butter or Allinson vege-butter in the saucepan in which the soup is to be made. When brown, add 4 pints of water, the celery washed and cut into pieces, the nutmeg, the pepper and salt. Let all cook until the celery is quite soft, then drain the liquid from the vegetables. Return it to the saucepan, boil the soup up, and add 1 oz. of vermicelli, sago, or Italian paste; let the soup cook until this is quite soft, and serve with sippets of crisp toast, or Allinson plain rusks.

CLEAR TOMATO SOUP

2 tablespoonfuls of tinned tomatoes, or 1 fair-sized fresh one, 1 small finely chopped and fried onion, a teaspoonful of vermicelli, pepper and salt to taste, 1/2 pint of water. Boil the tomatoes with the onion and water for 5 to 10 minutes, then drain all the liquid; return to the saucepan, season and sprinkle in the vermicelli, let the soup cook until the vermicelli is soft, and serve.

CREAM OF TOMATO SOUP

1 quart tomatoes
1/4 teaspoon soda
4 tablespoons butter
4 tablespoons flour
1 quart milk
1 tablespoon salt
1/2 teaspoon pepper

Stew tomatoes slowly one-half hour; rub through strainer; heat and add soda. In the meantime, melt butter and stir in flour; add milk slowly, cooking over low fire until thick; add seasoning. Take from fire and stir in hot tomatoes and serve immediately.

CREAM PEA SOUP

Soak three fourths of a pint of dried Scotch peas over night in a quart of water. In the morning put to cook in boiling water, cover closely and let them simmer gently four or five hours, or until the peas are very tender and well disintegrated; then rub through a colander to remove the skins. If the peas are very dry, add a little water or milk occasionally, to moisten them and facilitate the sifting. Just before the peas are done, prepare potatoes enough to make a pint and a half, after being cut in thin slices. Cook the potatoes until tender in a small amount of water, and rub them through a colander. Add the potatoes thus prepared to the sifted peas, and milk enough to make three and one half pints in all.

Return to the fire, and add a small head of celery cut finger lengths, and let the whole simmer together ten or fifteen minutes, until flavored. Remove the celery with a fork; add salt and a cup of thin cream. This should make about two quarts of soup. If preferred, the peas may be cooked without soaking. It will, however, require a little longer time.

CREAM BARLEY SOUP

Wash a cup of pearl barley, drain and simmer slowly in two quarts of water for four or five hours, adding boiling water from time to time as needed. When the barley is tender, strain off the liquor, of which there should be about three pints; add to it a portion of the cooked barley grains, salt, and a cup of whipped cream, and serve. If preferred, the beaten yolk of an egg may be used instead of cream.

CREAM OF CELERY SOUP

A pint of milk, a table-spoonful of flour, one of butter, a head of celery, a large slice of onion and small piece of nutmeg. Boil celery in a pint of water from thirty to forty-five minutes; boil nutmeg, onion and milk together. Mix flour with two tablespoonfuls of cold milk, and add to boiling milk. Cook ten minutes. Mash celery in the water in which it has been cooked, and stir into boiling milk. Add butter, and season with salt and pepper to taste. Strain and serve immediately. The flavor is improved by adding a cupful of whipped cream when the soup is in the tureen.

CREAM OF RICE SOUP

Two quarts of chicken stock (the water in which fowl have been boiled will answer), one tea-cupful of rice, a quart of cream or milk, a small onion, a stalk of celery and salt and pepper to taste. Wash rice carefully, and add to chicken stock, onion and celery. Cook slowly two hours (it should hardly bubble). Put through a sieve; add seasoning and the milk or cream, which has been allowed to come just to a boil.

CREAM OF ONION SOUP

Take 4 medium-sized onions, 4 Tb. butter, 2 Tb. flour, 2-1/2 c. milk, 1 tsp. salt and 1/8 tsp. pepper. Slice the onions and brown them in a frying pan with 2 tablespoonfuls of the butter. Make white sauce of the flour, the remaining butter, and the milk. Add to this the browned onions, salt, and pepper. Heat thoroughly and serve.

CHICKEN SOUP

Cut up the chicken; cut each joint, and let it boil an hour; make dumplings of a pint of milk, an egg, a little salt and flour, stirred in till quite stiff; drop this in, a spoonful at a time, while it is boiling; stir in a little thickening, with enough pepper, salt and parsley, to season the whole; let it boil a few minutes longer, and take it up in a tureen. Chopped celery is a great improvement to chicken soup; and new corn, cut off the cob, and put in when it is half done, gives it a very nice flavor.

CHICKEN CREAM SOUP

An old chicken for soup is much the best. Cut it up into quarters, put it into a soup kettle with half a pound of corned ham, and an onion; add four quarts of cold water. Bring slowly to a gentle boil, and keep this up until the liquid has diminished one-third, and the meat drops from the bones; then add half a cup of rice. Season with salt, pepper and a bunch of chopped parsley. Cook slowly until the rice is tender, then the meat should be taken out. Now stir in two cups of rich milk thickened with a little flour. The chicken could be fried in a spoonful of butter and gravy made, reserving some of the white part of the meat, chopping it and adding it to the soup.

CHICKEN CHEESE SOUP

Heat together 1-cup milk, 1-cup water in which 2 chicken bouillon cubes have been dissolved, and 1 can of condensed cream of chicken soup.

Stir in 1/4 cup grated American Cheddar cheese and season with salt, pepper, and plenty of paprika until cheese melts. Other popular American recipes simply add grated cheese to lima bean or split bean soup, peanut butter soup, or plain cheese soup with rice.

CHEESE SOUP

One and a half cupfuls of flour, one pint of rich cream, four tablespoonfuls of butter, four of grated Parmesan cheese, a speck of cayenne, two eggs, three quarts of clear soup stock.

Mix flour, cream, butter, cheese and pepper together. Place the basin in another of hot water and stir until the mixture becomes a smooth, firm paste. Break into it the two eggs, and mix quickly and thoroughly. Cook two minutes longer, and set away to cool. When cold, roll into little balls about the size of an American walnut. When the balls are all formed drop them into boiling water and cook gently five minutes; then put them in the soup tureen and pour the boiling stock on them. Pass a plate of finely grated Parmesan cheese with the soup.

CLAM SOUP

Mince two dozen hard shell clams very fine. Fry half a minced onion in an ounce of butter; add to it a pint of hot water, a pinch of nutmeg, four cloves, one allspice and six whole peppercorns.

Boil fifteen minutes and strain into a saucepan; add the chopped clams and a pint of clam-juice or hot water; simmer slowly two hours; strain and rub the pulp through a sieve into the liquid. Return it to the saucepan and keep it lukewarm. Boil three half-pints of milk in a saucepan (previously wet with cold water, which prevents burning) and whisk it into the soup.

Dissolve a teaspoonful of flour in cold milk, add it to the soup, taste for seasoning; heat it gently to near the boiling point; pour into a tureen previously heated with hot water, and serve with or without pieces of fried bread.

CHESTNUT SOUP

1 lb. chestnuts, 1-1/2 oz. nutter or butter, 2 tablespoons chopped parsley, 1 tablespoon wholemeal flour, 1-1/2 pints water.

First put on the chestnuts (without shelling or pricking) in cold water, and boil for an hour. Then remove shells and put the nuts in a saucepan with the fat. Fry for 10 minutes. Add the flour gradually, stirring all the time, then add the water. Cook gently for half an hour. Lastly, add the parsley, boil up, and serve. It is rather nicer if the flour is omitted, the necessary thickness being obtained by rubbing the soup through a sieve before adding the parsley. Those who do not object to milk may use 1-pint milk and 1-pint water in place of the 1-1/2 pints water.

CHESTNUT PUREE

Ingredients: 1 c. mashed chestnuts, 1 c. milk, 2 Tb. flour, 2 Tb. butter, 1 tsp. salt, 1/8 tsp. pepper, 1/8 tsp. celery salt and 1 c. white stock

Cook chestnuts for 10 minutes; then remove the shells and skins and mash the chestnuts. Make white sauce of the milk, flour, and butter. Add to this the mashed chestnuts, salt, pepper, celery salt, and stock. Heat thoroughly and serve.

CANNED GREEN PEA SOUP

Rub a can of green peas through a colander to remove the skins. Add a pint of milk and heat to boiling. If too thin, thicken with a little flour rubbed smooth in a very little cold milk. Season with salt and a half cup of cream. A small teaspoonful of white sugar may be added if desired. Green peas, instead of canned, may be used when procurable. When they have become a little too hard to serve alone, they can be used for soup, if thoroughly cooked.

CANNED CORN SOUP

Open a can of corn, turn it into a graniteware dish, and thoroughly mash with a potato-masher until each kernel is broken, then rub through a colander to remove the skins. Add sufficient rich milk to make the soup of the desired consistency, about one half pint for each pint can of corn will be needed. Season with salt, reheat, and serve. If preferred, a larger quantity of milk and some cream may be used, and the soup, when reheated, thickened with a little corn starch or flour. It may be turned through the colander a second time or not, as preferred.

CELERY SOUP

Chop quite fine enough fresh, crisp celery to make a pint, and cook it until tender in a very little boiling water. When done, heat three cupfuls of rich milk, part cream if it can be afforded, to boiling, add the celery, salt to season, and thicken the whole with a tablespoonful of flour rubbed smooth in a little cold milk; or add to the milk before heating a cupful of mashed potato, turn through a colander to remove lumps, reheat, add salt and the celery, and serve.

CODFISH SOUP

Take one-half pound of salt codfish that has been soaked, cut it up into squares, but not small. Prepare in a saucepan four tablespoons of good olive-oil, and one small onion cut into pieces. Cook the onion in the oil over a slow fire, without allowing the onion to become colored, then add a small bunch of parsley stems, a small piece of celery, a bay-leaf, and a small sprig of thyme. Cool for a few moments, then add two tomatoes, skinned and with the seeds removed, and cut into slices, two tablespoons of dry white wine, and one medium-sized potato, peeled and cut into slices, and, lastly, one cup of water. When the potato is half cooked, add the codfish, then one-half tablespoon more of olive-oil.

Remove the parsley stems, and put in instead one-half tablespoon of chopped-up parsley; add a good pinch of pepper, and some salt, if needed.

When the vegetables are thoroughly cooked pour the soup over pieces of toasted or fried bread, and serve.

COMBINATION SOUP

This soup is prepared from material already cooked, and requires two cups of cracked wheat, one and one half cups of Lima beans, one half cup of black beans, and one cup of stewed tomato. Rub the material together through a colander, adding, if needed, a little hot water to facilitate the sifting. Add boiling water to thin to the proper consistency, season with salt and if it can be afforded a little sweet cream,--the soup is, however, very palatable without the cream.

CURRY RICE SOUP

1 oz. rice, 1 pint milk and water (equal parts), 1 saltspoonful of curry, 1/4 oz. butter, 1 oz. finely chopped onion, salt to taste. Cook the rice with the onion, curry, and seasoning in the milk and water, until the rice is quite tender; add the butter, and serve.

CROUTONS FOR SOUP

In a frying pan have the depth of an inch of boiling fat; also have prepared slices of stale bread cut up into little half-inch squares; drop into the frying pan enough of these bits of bread to cover the surface of the fat. When browned, remove with a skimmer and drain; add to the hot soup and serve.

DRIED BEAN SOUP

Put two quarts of dried white beans to soak the night before you make the soup, which should be put on as early in the day as possible. Take two pounds of the lean of fresh beef (the coarse pieces will do). Cut them up and put them into your soup-pot with the bones belonging to them (which should be broken in pieces), and a pound of lean bacon, cut very small. If you have the remains of a piece of beef that has been roasted the day before, and so much underdone that the juices remain in it, you may put it into the pot and its bones along with it. Season the meat with pepper only, and pour on it six quarts of water. As soon as it boils, take off the scum, and put in the beans (having first drained them) and a head of celery cut small, or a tablespoonful of pounded celery seed. Boil it slowly till the meat is done to shreds, and the beans all dissolved. Then strain it through a colander into the tureen, and put into it small squares of toasted bread with the crust cut off.

DRIED WHITE BEANS SOUP

Dried beans should be soaked before boiling; they make very good soup with a small piece of bacon or salt pork boiled with them; put them to boil in plenty of water, and after they have boiled an hour, pour it off, and put in cold water and the meat or bones, and let them boil an hour longer; stir in a little thickening, with pepper, salt, parsley and thyme; mix up some dumplings, and drop in half an hour before the soup is done.

EEL SOUP

The small white Eels are the best. Having cut off their heads, skin the fish, and clean them, and cut them in three. To twelve small eel allow a pound and a half of chicken. Cut the chicken into small pieces, or slice it very thin, and scald it two or three times in boiling water, lest it be too salt. Chop together a bunch of parsley and some sweet marjoram stripped from the stalks. Put these ingredients into a soup kettle and season them with pepper: the checken will make it salt enough. Add a head of celery cut small, or a large table-spoonful of celery seed tied up in a bit of clear muslin to prevent its dispersing. Pat in two quarts of water, cover the kettle, and let it boil slowly till every thing is sufficiently done, and the fish and checken quite tender. Skim it frequently. Boil in another vessel a quart of rich milk, in which you have melted a quarter of a pound of butter divided into small bits and rolled in flour. Pour it hot to the soup, and stir in at the last the beaten yolks of four eggs. Give it another boil, just to take off the rawness of the eggs, and then put it into a tureen, taking out the bag of celery seed before you send the soup to table, and adding some toasted bread cut into small squares. In making toast for soap, cut the bread thick, and pare off all the crust.

EGG SOUP

Take 1 quart White Stock, 1 pint of Milk, 3 Yolks of Eggs, 1 oz. Sago, 1 Onion, Salt and Pepper as necessary. Boil the sago, stock, and onion together till the sago is clear; then take out the onion and season the soup with salt and pepper. Beat the yolks of the eggs in a basin, pour over the boiling milk, strain into the stock. Put over the fire and whisk till it comes to boiling point, but do not let it boil, or it may curdle. Pour into a tureen, sprinkle with chopped parsley, and send some fried bread to table with it.

EGG BALLS FOR SOUP

Take the yolks of six hard-boiled eggs and half a tablespoonful of wheat flour, rub them smooth with the yolks of two raw eggs and a teaspoonful of salt; mix all well together; make it in balls, and drop them into the boiling soup a few minutes before taking it up. Used in green turtle soup.

EGG DUMPLINGS FOR SOUP

To half a pint of milk put two well-beaten eggs, and as much wheat flour as will make a smooth, rather thick batter free from lumps; drop this batter, a tablespoonful at a time, into boiling soup.

FISH SOUP

Select a large, fine fish, clean it thoroughly, put it over the fire with a sufficient quantity of water, allowing for each pound of fish one quart of water; add an onion cut fine and a bunch of sweet herbs. When the fish is cooked, and is quite tasteless, strain all through a colander, return to the fire, add some butter, salt and pepper to taste. A small tablespoonful of Worcestershire sauce may be added if liked. Serve with small squares of fried bread and thin slices of lemon.

FISH CHOWDER

2 lb. fish, 1 small onion, 1 c. sliced potatoes, 1/2 c. stewed tomatoes, 1-1/2 tsp. salt, 1/8 tsp. pepper, 2 Tb. butter and 1-1/2 c. milk.

Skin the fish, remove the flesh, and cut it into small pieces. Simmer the head, bones, and skin of the fish and the onion in water for 1/2 hour.

Strain, and add to this stock the fish, potatoes, tomatoes, salt, and pepper. Simmer together until the potatoes are soft. Add the butter and milk. Serve over crackers.

FRENCH SOUP

1 small onion chopped fine, 1 oz. of cheese shredded fine, 1 slice of dry toast, 3/4 pint of water, a little milk, pepper and salt to taste. Break up the toast, and set all the ingredients over the fire; cook till the onion is tender, add 1/2 gill of milk, and serve.

FRENCH CABBAGE SOUP

1 medium-sized cabbage, 1 lb. of potatoes, 1 oz. of butter, 3 pints of milk and water equal parts, pepper and salt to taste, 1 dessertspoonful of finely chopped parsley, and 2 blades of nutmeg, and 1 dessertspoonful of Allinson fine wheat meal. Wash the cabbage and shred it finely, peel the potatoes and cut them into small dice; boil the vegetables in the milk and water until quite tender, adding the nutmeg, butter, and seasoning. When quite soft, rub the wheat meal smooth with a little water, let it simmer with the soup for 5 minutes, add the parsley, and serve.

FRENCH ONION SOUP

1/2 lb. onions, 3 oz. grated cheese, 2 oz. butter, some squares of whole meal bread, pepper and salt to taste. Peel and chop the onions, and fry them a nice brown in the butter. When brown add to it the cheese and 3 pints of water. Boil all up together and season to taste. Place the bread in the tureen, pour the boiling soup over it, and serve.

FORCEMEAT BALLS FOR SOUP

1 Tb. butter, 1 small onion, 1-1/2 c. bread, without crusts, 1 egg, 1 tsp. salt, 1/2 tsp. pepper, Dash of nutmeg, 1 Tb. chopped parsley and 1/2 c. sausage meat. Melt the butter in a saucepan and add the onion finely chopped. Fry for several minutes over the fire. Soak the bread in water until thoroughly softened and then squeeze out all the water. Mix with the bread the egg, salt, pepper, nutmeg, parsley, and meat, and to this add also the butter and fried onion. Form small balls of this mixture and sauté them in shallow fat, fry them in deep fat, or, after brushing them over with fat, bake them in the oven. Place a few in each serving of soup.

GREEN CORN SOUP

Take six well-filled ears of tender green corn. Run a sharp knife down the rows and split each grain; then with the back of a knife, scraping from the large to the small end of the ear, press out the pulp, leaving the hulls on the cob. Break the cobs if long, put them in cold water sufficient to cover, and boil half an hour. Strain off the water, of which there should be at least one pint. Put the corn water on again, and when boiling add the corn pulp, and cook fifteen minutes, or until the raw taste is destroyed. Rub through a rather coarse colander, add salt and a pint of hot unskimmed milk; if too thin, thicken with a little cornstarch or flour, boil up, and serve. If preferred, a teaspoonful of sugar may be added to the soup. A small quantity of cooked macaroni, cut in rings, makes a very pretty and palatable addition to the soup. The soup is also excellent flavored with celery.

GREEN PEA SOUP

Gently simmer two quarts of shelled peas in sufficient water to cook, leaving almost no juice when tender. Rub through a colander, moistening if necessary with a little cold milk. Add to the sifted peas an equal quantity of rich milk and a small onion cut in halves. Boil all together five or ten minutes until the soup is delicately flavored, then remove the onion with a skimmer; add salt if desired, and serve. If preferred, a half-cup of thin cream may be added just before serving. Celery may be used in place of the onion, or both may be omitted.

GREEN PEAS SOUP

Take four pounds of knuckle of veal, and a pound of bacon. Cut them to pieces, and put them into a soup kettle with a sprig of mint and four quarts of water. Boil it moderately fast, and skim it well. When the meat is boiled to rags, strain it out, and put to the liquor a quart of young green peas. Boil them till they are entirely dissolved, and till they have thickened the soup, and given it a green color. You may greatly improve the color by pounding a handful of spinach in a mortar, straining the juice, and adding it to the soup about a quarter of an hour before it has done boiling. Have ready two quarts of green peas that have been boiled in another pot with a sprig of mint, and two or three lumps of loaf sugar, (which will greatly improve the taste.) After they have boiled in this pot twenty minutes, take out the mint, put the whole peas into the pot of soup, and boil all together about ten minutes. Then put it into a tureen, and send it to table.

GREEN BEAN SOUP

Prepare a quart of fresh string beans by pulling off ends and strings and breaking into small pieces. Boil in a small quantity of water. If the beans are fresh and young, three pints will be sufficient; if wilted or quite old, more will be needed, as they will require longer cooking. There should be about a teacupful and a half of liquid left when the beans are perfectly tender and boiled in pieces. Rub through a colander, return to the kettle, and for each cup of the bean pulp add salt, a cup and a half of unskimmed milk; boil together for a few minutes, thicken with a little flour, and serve. The quart of beans should be sufficient for three pints of soup.

GREEN TURTLE SOUP

One turtle, two onions, a bunch of sweet herbs, juice of one lemon, five quarts of water, a glass of Madeira.

After removing the entrails, cut up the coarser parts of the turtle meat and bones. Add four quarts of water, and stew four hours with the herbs, onions, pepper and salt. Stew very slowly; do not let it cease boiling during this time. At the end of four hours strain the soup, and add the finer parts of the turtle and the green fat, which has been simmered one hour in two quarts of water. Thicken with brown flour; return to the soup-pot, and simmer gently for an hour longer. If there are eggs in the turtle, boil them in a separate vessel for four hours, and throw into the soup before taking up. If not, put in force meatballs; then the juice of the lemon, and the wine; beat up at once and pour out. Some cooks add the finer meat before straining, boiling all together five hours; then strain, thicken and put in the green fat, cut into lumps an inch long. This makes a handsomer soup than if the meat is left in.

GROUSE SOUP

The bones of two roasted grouse and the breast of one, a quart of any kind of stock, or pieces and bones of cold roasts; three quarts of cold water, two slices of turnip, two of carrot, two large onions, two cloves, two stalks of celery, a bouquet of sweet herbs, three tablespoonfuls of butter, three of flour. Cook the grouse bones in three quarts of water four hours. The last hour add the vegetables and the cloves; then strain, and return to the lire with the quart of stock. Cook the butter and the flour together until a rich brown, and then turn into the stock. Cut the breast of the grouse into very small pieces and add to the soup. Season with salt and pepper and simmer gently half an hour. If there is any fat on the soup, skim it off. Serve with fried bread. When bones and meat are used instead of the stock, use one more quart of water, and cook them with the grouse bones.

GIBLET SOUP

The giblets from two or three fowl or chickens, any kind of stock, or if there are remains of the roast chickens, use these; one large onion, two slices of carrot, one of turnip, two stalks of celery, two quarts of water, one of stock, two large table-spoonfuls of butter, two of flour, salt, pepper. Put the giblets on to boil in the two quarts of water, and boil gently until reduced to one quart (it will take about two hours); then take out the giblets. Cut all the hard, tough parts from the gizzards, and put hearts, livers and gizzards together and chop rather coarse.

Return them to the liquor in which they were boiled, and add the quart of stock. Have the vegetables cut fine, and fry them in the butter until they are very tender (about fifteen minutes), but be careful they do not burn; then add the dry flour to them and stir until the flour browns.

Turn this mixture into the soup, and season with pepper and salt. Cook gently half an hour and serve with toasted bread. If the chicken bones are used, put them on to boil in three quarts of water, and boil the giblets with them.

GUMBO SOUP

Take two pounds fresh beef; put this in a dinner-pot, with two gallons of water; after boiling two hours, throw in a quarter of a peck of ocra, cut into small slices, and about a quart of ripe tomatoes, peeled and cut up; slice four or five large onions; fry them brown, and dust in while they are frying from your dredge box, several spoonfuls of flour; add these, with pepper, salt and parsley, or other herbs, to your taste, about an hour before the soup is finished; it will require six hours moderate boiling.

HARICOT SOUP

1 lb. of haricot beans, 1/2 lb. of onions, 1 lb. of turnips, 2 carrots, 2 sticks of celery, 1 teaspoonful of mixed herbs, 1/2 oz. of parsley, 1 oz. of butter, 2 quarts of water, pepper and salt to taste. Cut up the vegetables and set them to boil in the water with the haricot beans (which should have been steeped over night in cold water), adding the butter, herbs, and seasoning. Cook all very gently for 3-1/2 to 4 hours, stirring occasionally. When the beans are quite tender, rub the soup through a sieve, adding more water if needed; return it to the saucepan, add the parsley chopped up finely, boil it up and serve.

HARICOT BEAN SOUP

2 heaped breakfast-cups beans, 2 qts. Water, 3 tablespoons chopped parsley or 1/2 lb. tomatoes, nut or dairy butter size of walnut, 1 tablespoon lemon juice.

For this soup use the small white or brown haricots. Soak overnight in 1 qt. of the water. In the morning add the rest of the water, and boil until soft. It may then be rubbed through a sieve, but this is not imperative. Add the chopped parsley, the lemon juice, and the butter. Boil up and serve. If tomato pulp is preferred for flavoring instead of parsley, skin the tomatoes and cook slowly to pulp (without water) before adding.

ITALIAN SOUP

Take 2 oz. Macaroni, 2 quarts Water or Pot Boilings, 2 Tomatoes, 1 oz. Butter and 2 oz. Cheese Rind. Put the water or stock on to boil, and when it boils put in the macaroni and boil from twenty-five to thirty minutes. While it is boiling grate up a dry piece of cheese. Put the tomatoes into boiling water and remove the skin, slice them up and put them into a saucepan with the butter and some pepper and salt, and cook them for a few minutes. When the macaroni is soft, cut it into pieces one inch long, put a layer of tomatoes at the bottom of the soup tureen, then a layer of grated cheese, then one of macaroni; repeat this until all the materials are used up, pour over it boiling the liquor in which the macaroni has been cooked, cover down for a few minutes, and serve.

IRISH POTATO SOUP

Peel and boil eight medium-sized potatoes with a large onion sliced, some herbs, salt and pepper; press all through a colander; then thin it with rich milk and add a lump of butter, more seasoning, if necessary; let it heat well and serve hot.

JULIENNE SOUP

Cut carrots and turnips into quarter-inch piece the shape of dice; also celery into thin slices. Cover them with boiling water; add a teaspoonful of salt, half a teaspoonful pepper, and cook until soft. In another saucepan have two quarts of boiling stock, to which add the cooked vegetables, the water and more seasoning if necessary. Serve hot. In the spring and summer season use asparagus, peas and string beans - all cut into small uniform thickness.

The day before needed, put two pounds of beef cut from the lower part of the round, into two quarts of cold water and let come slowly to the boil, skimming carefully until perfectly clear. When this point is reached, add a small onion, two stalks of celery, two cloves, and keep at the boiling point for seven hours; then strain into an earthen bowl and let cool until next day. A half hour before needed, skim off all the fat, add pepper and salt to taste; also a half pint of mixed vegetables which have been cooked in salted water and cut in uniform dice shape. Let come to a boil, and serve.

KIDNEY SOUP

Take 1 Ox Kidney, 2 Onions, 1 oz. Butter, 1 oz. Corn flour, 2 quarts Stock, Salt, Lemon Juice and parsley as necessary. Slice up the onions and fry them in the butter, strain them out and return the butter to the saucepan. Stir in the corn flour, and when well mixed pour over the stock and stir until it boils. Slice the kidney up into small pieces, and put it in; simmer very gently for one hour. Just before serving, season with salt and a little lemon juice; pour into a tureen and sprinkle a little chopped parsley on top. This soup must be cooked very slowly, or the kidney will be hard and tough.

KORNLET SOUP

Kornlet or canned green corn pulp, may be made into a most appetizing soup in a few minutes by adding to a pint of kornlet an equal quantity of rich milk, heating to boiling, and thickening it with a teaspoonful of flour rubbed smooth in a little cold milk.

KORNLET AND TOMATO SOUP.

Put together equal quantities of kornlet and strained stewed tomato, season with salt and heat to boiling; add for each quart one fourth to one half cup of hot thin cream, thicken with a tablespoonful of flour rubbed smooth in a little water, and serve. Cooked corn rubbed through a colander may also be used for this soup.

LENTIL SOUP

Simmer a pint of lentils in water until tender. If desired to have the soup less dark in color and less strong in flavor, the lentils may be first parboiled for a half hour, and then drained and put into fresh boiling water. Much valuable nutriment is thus lost, however. When perfectly tender, mash through a colander to remove all skins; add salt and a cup of thin cream, and it too thick, sufficient boiling milk or water to thin to the proper consistency, heat again to boiling, and serve. If preferred, an additional quantity of liquid may be added and the soup slightly thickened with browned flour.

Stew for 2 hours more. Then rub through a sieve, or not, as preferred. Add the lemon juice, herb powder, and butter (nut or dairy), and serve.

LENTIL AND PARSNIP SOUP

Cook together one pint of lentils and one half a small parsnip, sliced, until tender in a small quantity of boiling water. When done, rub through a colander, and add boiling water to make a soup of the proper consistency. Season with salt and if desired a little cream.

LETTUCE SOUP

Take 1 small lettuce, Meat stock, 2 potatoes, The leaves of a head of celery, 2 tablespoons of peas, fresh or canned, 1 heaping tablespoon of flour. Put the potatoes, cold boiled, into the stock when it boils, add the celery leaves, the lettuce chopped up, the peas, and the flour mixed well with a little cold stock or water. Boil for one hour and a half, and serve with little squares of fried bread.

LENTEN SOUP

Take 6 Onions, 2 oz. Butter or Beef Dripping, 2 quarts of Water or Pot Liquor, Crusts of Bread, Salt and Pepper as necessary. Peel and slice up the onions and put them into a saucepan with the butter or dripping, and brown them. Then let them cook, covered over, for an hour.

Break in some brown dry crusts of bread. Pour over the boiling liquor the water in which some vegetables, such as carrots, turnips, or cauliflowers, have been boiled, stir it well and boil for an hour; rub through a sieve. If it is not thick enough, let it boil again without the lid for ten minutes. Season well with pepper and salt, and serve.

LIMA BEAN SOUP

Simmer a pint of Lima beans gently in just sufficient water to cook and not burn, until they have fallen to pieces. Add more boiling water as needed. When done, rub the beans through a colander. Add rich milk or water to make of the proper consistency, and salt to season; reheat and serve. White beans may be used in place of Lima beans, but they require more prolonged cooking. A heaping tablespoonful of pearl tapioca or sago previously soaked in cold water, may be added to the soup when it is reheated, if liked, and the whole cooked until the sago is transparent.

LEEK SOUP

2 bunches of leeks, 1-1/2 pints of milk, 1 oz. of butter, 1 lb. of potatoes, pepper and salt to taste, and the juice of a lemon. Cut off the coarse part of the green ends of the leeks, and cut the leeks lengthways, so as to be able to brush out the grit. Wash the leeks well, and see no grit remains, then cut them in short pieces. Peel, wash, and cut up the potatoes, then cook both vegetables with 2 pints of water. When the vegetables are quite tender, rub them through a sieve. Return the mixture to the saucepan, add the butter, milk, and seasoning, and boil the soup up again. Before serving add the lemon juice; serve with sippets of toast.

LOBSTER SOUP

Have ready a good broth made of three pounds of veal boiled slowly in as much water as will cover it, till the meat is reduced to shreds. It must then be well strained.

Having boiled one fine middle-sized lobster, extract all the meat from the body and claws. Bruise part of the coral in a mortar, and also an equal quantity of the meat. Mix them well together. Add nutmeg, cayenne, salt and pepper, and make them up into force meat balls, binding the mixture with the yolk of an egg slightly beaten. Take three quarts of the veal broth and put it into the meat of the lobster cut into mouthfuls. Boil it together about twenty minutes.

Then thicken it with the remaining coral (which you must first rub through a sieve), and add the force meat balls and a little butter rolled in flour. Simmer it gently for ten minutes, but do not let it come to a boil, as that will injure the color. Serve with small dice of bread fried brown in butter.

LOBSTER SOUP WITH MILK

Meat of a small lobster, chopped fine; three crackers, rolled fine, butter size of an egg, salt and pepper to taste and a speck of cayenne. Mix all in the same pan, and add, gradually, a pint of boiling milk, stirring all the while. Boil up once, and serve.

MACARONI SOUP

Heat a quart of milk, to which has been added a tablespoonful of finely grated bread crust (the brown part only, from the top of the loaf) and a slice of onion to flavor, in a double boiler.

When the milk is well flavored, remove the onion, turn through a colander, add salt, and thicken with two teaspoonfuls of flour rubbed smooth in a little cold milk. Lastly add one cupful of cooked macaroni, and serve.

MILK SOUP

Boil two quarts of milk with a quarter of a pound of sweet almonds, and two ounces of bitter ones, blanched and broken to pieces, and a large stick of cinnamon broken up. Stir in sugar enough to make it very sweet. When it has boiled strain it. Cut some thin slices of bread, and (having pared off the crust) toast them. Lay them in the bottom of a tureen, pour a little of the hot milk over them, and cover them close, that they may soak. Beat the yolks of five eggs very light Set the milk on hot coals, and add the eggs to it by degrees; stirring it all the time till it thickens. Then take it off instantly, lest it curdle, and pour it into the tureen, boiling hot, over the bread. This will be still better if you cover the bottom with slices of baked apple.

MILK SOUP FOR CHILDREN

1-1/2 pints of milk, 1 egg, 1 tablespoonful of Allinson fine wheat meal, 1-1/2 oz. of sultanas, sugar to taste. Boil 1-1/4 pints of milk, add the sugar, beat up the egg with the rest of the milk and mix the wheat meal smooth with it; stir this into the boiling milk, add the sultanas, and let the soup simmer for 10 minutes.

MUSHROOM SOUP

2 oz. mushrooms cut up small, 1/2 small onion chopped fine, 1 dessertspoonful of fine wheatmeal, pepper and salt, 1/2 oz. of butter, a little milk. Stew the mushrooms and onions together in the butter until well cooked, add 1/2 pint of water, and cook the vegetables for 10 minutes. Add seasoning, and the meal smoothed in a little milk. Let the soup thicken and boil up, and serve with sippets of toast.

MULLIGATAWNY SOUP

Take 2 quarts Stock, 1 Apple, 1 Onion, 1 Carrot, 1/2 oz. Curry Powder, 1 oz. Flour and 1 oz. Butter. The liquor in which poultry or a rabbit has been boiled is the best for this soup. Slice up the apple, onion, and carrot, and fry them in the butter; sprinkle over the curry powder and flour and brown that too; pour over the boiling stock and stir until it boils up, simmer gently for one hour, then rub through a sieve and return to the saucepan. Bring to the boil, flavour with salt and lemon juice. Pour into a warm tureen and serve. Send well-boiled rice to the table with this soup.

MEAT BALLS FOR SOUP

One cupful of cooked veal or fowl meat, minced; mix with this a handful of fine bread crumbs, the yolks of four hard-boiled eggs rubbed smooth together with a tablespoon of milk; season with pepper and salt; add a half teaspoon of flour, and bind all together with two beaten eggs; the hands to be well floured, and the mixture to be made into little balls the size of a nutmeg; drop into the soup about twenty minutes before serving.

NOODLE SOUP

To make a good stock for noodle soup, take a small shank of beef, one of mutton, and another of veal; have the bones cracked and boil them together for twenty-four hours. Put with them two good-sized potatoes, a carrot, a turnip, an onion, and some celery. Salt and pepper to taste.

If liked, a bit of bay leaf may be added. When thoroughly well done, strain through a colander and set aside until required for use. For the noodles, use one egg for an ordinary family, and more in proportion to quantity required. Break the eggs into the flour, add a little salt, and mix into a rather stiff dough. Roll very thin and cut into fine bits. Let them dry for two hours, then drop them into the boiling stock about ten minutes before serving.

NOODLES FOR SOUP

Beat up one egg light, add a pinch of salt, and flour enough to make a very stiff dough; roll out very thin, like thin pie crust, dredge with flour to keep from sticking. Let it remain on the breadboard to dry for an hour or more; then roll it up into a tight scroll, like a sheet of music.

Begin at the end and slice it into slips as thin as straws. After all are cut, mix them lightly together, and to prevent them sticking, keep them floured a little until you are ready to drop them into your soup which should be done shortly before dinner, for if boiled too long they will go to pieces.

ONION SOUP

One quart of milk, six large onions, yolks of four eggs, three tablespoonfuls of butter, a large one of flour, one cupful of cream, salt, pepper. Put the butter in a frying-pan. Cut the onions into thin slices and drop in the butter. Stir until they begin to cook; then cover tight and set back where they will simmer, but not burn, for half an hour. Now put the milk on to boil, and then add the dry flour to the onions, and stir constantly for three minutes over the fire. Then turn the mixture into the milk and cook fifteen minutes. Rub the soup through a strainer, return to the fire, season with salt and pepper. Beat the yokes of the eggs well; add the cream to them and stir into the soup. Cook three minutes, stirring constantly. If you have no cream, use milk, in which case add a tablespoonful of butter at the same time.

OATMEAL SOUP

6 oz. of coarse oatmeal, the outer part of a head of celery, 1 Spanish onion, 1 turnip, 1 oz. of butter, and pepper and salt. Wash and cut the vegetables up small, set them over the fire with 2 quarts of water. When boiling, stir in the oatmeal and allow all to cook gently for 2 hours. Rub the mixture well through a sieve, adding hot water it necessary. Return the soup to the saucepan, add the butter and pepper and salt, and let it boil up. The soup should be of a smooth, creamy consistency. Serve with sippets of toast or Allinson plain rusks.

OKRA SOUP

One cold roast chicken, two quarts of stock (any kind), one of water, quarter of a pound of salt pork, one quart of green okra, an onion, salt, pepper, three table-spoonfuls of flour. Cut the okra pods into small pieces. Slice the pork and onion. Fry the pork, and then add the onion and okra. Cover closely, and fry half an hour. Cut all the meat from the chicken. Put the bones on with the water. Add the okra and onion, first being careful to press out all the pork fat possible. Into the fat remaining put the flour, and stir until it becomes a rich brown; add this to the other ingredients. Cover the pot, and simmer three hours; then rub through a sieve, and add the stock, salt and pepper and the meat of the chicken, cut into small pieces. Simmer gently twenty minutes. Serve with a dish of boiled rice.

OX-TAIL SOUP

Two ox-tails, two slices of beef, one ounce of butter, two carrots, two turnips, three onions, one leek, one head of celery, one bunch of savory herbs, pepper, a tablespoonful of salt, two tablespoonfuls of catsup, one-half glass of port wine, three quarts of water. Cut up the tails, separating them at the joints; wash them, and put them in a stew pan with the butter. Cut the vegetables and beef in slices and add them with the herbs. Put in one-half pint of water, and stir it over a quick fire till the juices are drawn. Fill up the stew pan with water, and, when boiling, add the salt. Skim well, and simmer very gently for four hours, or until the tails are tender. Take them out, skim and strain the soup, thicken with flour, and flavor with the catsup and port wine. Put back the tails; simmer for five minutes and serve.

OYSTER SOUP

Two quarts of oysters, one quart of milk, two tablespoonfuls of butter, one teacupful of hot water; pepper, salt. Strain all the liquor from the oysters; add the water, and heat. When near the boil, add the seasoning, then the oysters. Cook about five minutes from the time they begin to simmer, until they "ruffle." Stir in the butter, cook one minute, and pour into the tureen. Stir in the boiling milk and send to table. Some prefer all water in place of milk.

OYSTER SOUP -2

Scald one gallon of oysters in their own liquor. Add one quart of rich milk to the liquor, and when it comes to a boil, skim out the oysters and set aside. Add the yolks of four eggs, two good tablespoonfuls of butter, and one of flour, all mixed well together, but in this order - first, the milk, then, after beating the eggs, add a little of the hot liquor to them gradually, and stir them rapidly into the soup. Lastly, add the butter and whatever seasoning you fancy besides plain pepper and salt, which must both be put in to taste with caution. Celery salt most persons like extremely; others would prefer a little marjoram or thyme; others again nutmeg and a bit of onion. Use your own discretion in this regard.

PARSNIP SOUP -1.

Take a quart of well scraped, thinly sliced parsnips, one cup of bread crust shavings (prepared as for Brown Soup), one head of celery, one small onion, and one pint of sliced potatoes. The parsnips used should be young and tender, so that they will cook in about the same length of time as the other vegetables. Use only sufficient water to cook them. When done, rub through a colander and add salt and sufficient rich milk, part cream if desired, to make of the proper consistency. Reheat and serve.

PARSNIP SOUP -2.

Wash, pare, and slice equal quantities of parsnips and potatoes. Cook, closely covered, in a small quantity of water until soft. If the parsnips are not young and tender, they must be put to cook first, and the potatoes added when they are half done. Mash through a colander. Add salt, and milk to make of the proper consistency, season with cream, reheat and serve.

PEA AND TOMATO SOUP

Soak one pint of Scotch peas over night. When ready to cook, put into a quart of boiling water and simmer slowly until quite dry and well disintegrated. Rub through a colander to remove the skins. Add a pint of hot water, one cup of mashed potato, two cups of strained stewed tomato, and one cup of twelve-hour cream. Turn into a double-boiler and cook together for a half hour or longer; turn a second time through a colander or soup strainer and serve. The proportions given are quite sufficient for two quarts of soup. There may need to be some variation in the quantity of tomato to be used, depending upon its thickness. If very thin, a larger quantity and less water will be needed. The soup should be a rich reddish brown in color when done. The peas may be cooked without being first soaked, if preferred.

PEAS SOUP

4 cups split peas, 1 carrot, 1 turnip, 2 onions, 4 qts. Water, 4 sticks celery, 2 teaspoons herb powder, 1 tablespoon lemon juice, 1 oz. butter.

Soak the split peas overnight. Stew the peas very gently in the water for 2 hours, taking off any scum that rises. Well wash the vegetables, slice them, and add to the soup. Stew for 2 hours more. Then rub through a sieve, or not, as preferred. Add the lemon juice, herb powder, and butter (nut or dairy), and serve.

PEARS SOUP

1 lb. pears, 1 qt. water, sugar and flavoring, 1 tablespoon sago.

Wash the pears and cut into quarters, but do not peel or core. Put into a saucepan with the water and sugar and flavouring to taste. When sweet, ripe pears can be obtained, people with natural tastes will prefer no addition of any kind. Otherwise, a little cinnamon, cloves, or the yellow part of lemon rind may be added. Stew until the pears are soft. Strain through a sieve, rubbing the pear pulp through, but leaving cores, etc., behind. Wash the sago, add to the strained soup, and boil gently for 1 hour. Stir now and then, as the sago is apt to stick to the pan.

PLUM SOUP

1 lb. plum, 1 qt. water, sugar and flavoring, 1-tablespoon sago.

Wash the plums and cut into quarters, but do not peel or core. Put into a saucepan with the water and sugar and flavoring to taste. When sweet, ripe plums can be obtained, people with natural tastes will prefer no addition of any kind. Otherwise, a little cinnamon, cloves, or the yellow part of lemon rind may be added. Stew until the plums are soft. Strain through a sieve, rubbing the plum pulp through, but leaving cores, etc., behind. Wash the sago, add to the strained soup, and boil gently for 1 hour. Stir now and then, as the sago is apt to stick to the pan.

POTATO SOUP -1.

Peel thinly 2 lbs. potatoes. (A floury kind should be used for this soup.) Cut into small pieces, and put into a saucepan with enough water to cover them. Add three large onions (sliced), unless tomatoes are preferred for flavoring. Bring to the boil, then simmer until the potatoes are cooked to a mash. Rub through a sieve or beat with a fork. Now add 3/4 pint water or 1 pint milk, and a little nutmeg if liked. Boil up and serve. If the milk is omitted, the juice and pulp of two or three tomatoes may be added, and the onions may be left out also.

POTATO SOUP -2.

For each quart of soup required, cook a pint of sliced potatoes in sufficient water to cover them. When tender, rub through a colander. Return to the fire, and add enough rich, sweet milk, part cream if it can be afforded to make a quart in all, and a little salt. Let the soup come to a boil, and add a teaspoonful of flour or corn starch, rubbed to a paste with a little water; boil a few minutes and serve. A cup and a half of cold mashed potato or a pint of sliced baked potato can be used instead of fresh material; in which case add the milk and heat before rubbing through the colander. A slice of onion or a stalk of celery may be simmered in the soup for a few minutes to flavor, and then removed with a skimmer or a spoon. A good mixed potato soup is made by using one third sweet and two thirds Irish potatoes, in the same manner as above.

POTATO SOUP -3.

2 lbs. of potatoes, 1/2 stick of celery or the outer stalks of a head of celery, saving the heart for table use; 1 large Spanish onion, 1 pint of milk, 1 oz. of butter, a heaped up tablespoonful of finely chopped parsley, and pepper and salt to taste. Peel, wash, and cut in pieces the potatoes, peel and chop roughly the onion, prepare and cut in small pieces the celery. Cook the vegetables in three pints of water until they are quite soft. Rub them through a sieve, return the fluid mixture to the saucepan; add the milk, butter, and seasoning, and boil the soup up again; if too thick add more water. Mix the parsley in the soup just before serving.

POTATO CHOWDER

1-1/2 c. sliced potatoes, 1 small onion, sliced, 1 c. water, 1-1/2 c. milk, 1 tsp. salt

1/8 tsp. pepper and 2 Tb. butter.

Cook the potatoes and onion in the water until they are soft, but not soft enough to fall to pieces. Rub half of the potatoes through a sieve and return to the sliced ones. Add the milk, salt, pepper, and butter. Cook together for a few minutes and serve.

POTATO AND RICE SOUP

Cook a quart of sliced potatoes in as little water as possible. When done, rub through a colander. Add salt, a quart of rich milk, and reheat. If desired, season with a slice of onion, a stalk of celery, or a little parsley. Just before serving, add a half cup of cream and a cup and a half of well-cooked rice with unbroken grains. Stir gently and serve at once.

POTATO AND VERMICELLI SOUP

Breakup a cupful of vermicelli and drop into boiling water. Let it cook for ten or fifteen minutes, and then turn into a colander to drain. Have ready a potato soup prepared the same as in the proceeding; stir the vermicelli lightly into it just before serving.

PLAIN RICE SOUP

Wash and pick over four tablespoonfuls of rice, put it in an earthen dish with a quart of water, and place in a moderate oven. When the water is all absorbed, add a quart of rich milk, and salt if desired; turn into a granite kettle and boil ten minutes, or till the rice is done. Add a half cup of sweet cream and serve. A slice of onion or stalk of celery can be boiled with the soup after putting in the kettle, and removed before serving, if desired to flavor.

PEA SOUP -1.

1 lb. of split peas, 1 lb. of potatoes, peeled, washed, and cut into pieces, 1 Spanish onion, 1 carrot, 1 turnip, 1/2 head of celery or a whole small one, 1 oz. of butter, pepper and salt to taste, Pick and wash the peas, and set them to boil in 2 quarts of water. Add the potatoes and the other vegetables, previously prepared and cut into small pieces, the butter and seasoning. When all the ingredients are soft, rub them through a sieve and return them to the saucepan. If the soup is too thick, add more water. Boil it up, and serve with fresh chopped mint, or fried dice of Allinson wholemeal bread. Allow 3 to 4 hours for the soup.

PEA SOUP -2.

Put a quart of dried peas into five quarts of water; boil for four hours; then add three or four large onions, two heads of celery, a carrot, two turnips, all cut up rather fine. Season with pepper and salt. Boil two hours longer, and if the soup becomes too thick add more water. Strain through a colander and stir in a tablespoonful of cold butter. Serve hot, with small pieces of toasted bread placed in the bottom of the tureen.

PHILADELPHIA PEPPER POT

Put two pounds of tripe and four calves' feet into the soup-pot and cover them with cold water; add a red pepper, and boil closely until the calves' feet are boiled very tender; take out the meat, skim the liquid, stir it, cut the tripe into small pieces, and put it back into the liquid; if there is not enough liquid, add boiling water; add half a teaspoonful of sweet marjoram, sweet basil, and thyme, two sliced onions, sliced potatoes, salt. When the vegetables have boiled until almost tender, add a piece of butter rolled in flour, drop in some egg balls, and boil fifteen minutes more. Take up and serve hot.

PHILADELPHIA CLAM SOUP

Twenty-five small clams, one quart of milk, half a cupful of butter, one table-spoonful of chopped parsley, three potatoes, two large tablespoonfuls of flour, salt, pepper. The clams should be chopped fine end put into a colander to drain. Pare the potatoes, and chop rather fine. Put them on to boil with the milk, in a double kettle. Rub the butter and flour together until perfectly creamy, and when the milk and potatoes have been boiling fifteen minutes, stir this in, and cook eight minutes more. Add the parsley, pepper and salt, and cook three minutes longer. Now add the clams. Cook one minute longer, and serve. This gives a very delicate soup, as the liquor from the clams is not used.

PORTUGUESE SOUP

4 onions, 4 tomatoes, 1 oz. of grated cheese, 1/4 lb. of stale Allinson whole meal bread, 1 quart of water, 1 oz. of butter, 1 even teaspoonful of herbs, pepper and salt to taste. Slice the onions and fry them until brown, add the tomatoes skinned and sliced, the water, herbs, and pepper and salt, and let the whole boil gently for 1 hour. Cut up the bread into dice, and put it into the tureen, pour the soup over it, cover, and let it stand for 10 minutes to allow the bread to soak; sprinkle the cheese over before serving.

PUMPKIN SOUP

Two pounds of pumpkin. Take out seeds and pare off the rind. Cut into small pieces, and put into a stew-pan with half a pint of water. Simmer slowly an hour and a half, then rub through a sieve and put back on the fire with one and a half pints of boiling milk, butter the size of an egg, one tea-spoonful of sugar, salt and pepper to taste, and three slices of stale bread, cut into small squares. Stir occasionally; and when it boils, serve.

RICE SOUP

3 oz. of rice, 4 oz. of grated cheese, a breakfast cupful of tomato juice, 1 oz. of butter, pepper and salt to taste. Boil the rice till tender in 2-1/2 pints of water, with the butter and seasoning. When quite soft, add the tomato juice and the cheese; stir until the soup boils and the cheese is dissolved, and serve. If too much of the water has boiled away, add a little more.

RICE CHEESE SOUP

1 cup of rice, 3/4 pint water, 1/4 pint milk, 1 oz. grated cheese, 1/4 oz. butter, seasoning to taste. Cook the rice in the milk and water until tender, then add the cheese, butter, and seasoning, and let the soup boil up until the cheese is dissolved.

RICE AND GREEN-PEA SOUP

2 oz. of rice, 1 breakfast cupful of shelled green peas, 1 pint of milk, 1 quart of water, 1 oz. of butter. Boil the rice in the water for 10 minutes, add the peas, the butter and pepper and salt to taste. Let it cook until the rice and peas are tender, add the milk and boil the soup up before serving.

RICE AND ONION SOUP

4 onions, 3 oz. of rice, 1-1/2 oz. of butter, 3 pints of water, pepper and salt. Chop the onions up very finely, and fry them with the butter until slightly browned; add the rice, seasoning, and water, and let the whole cook gently until quite soft. A tablespoonful of finely chopped parsley may be added.

ST. ANDREW'S SOUP

4 large potatoes, 1 pint of clear tomato juice (from tinned tomatoes), 1 pint of milk, 1 pint of water, 2 eggs, 1 oz. of butter, seasoning to taste.

Boil the potatoes in their skins; when tender peel and pass them through a potato masher. Put the potatoes into a saucepan with the butter, tomato juice, and water, adding pepper and salt to taste. Allow the soup to simmer for 10 minutes, then add the milk; boil up again, remove the saucepan to the cool side of the stove and stir in the eggs well beaten. Serve at once with sippets of toast, or Allinson plain rusks.

SCARLET RUNNER SOUP

1-1/2 lbs. of French beans or scarlet runners, 1 onion, 1 carrot, 1 stick of celery, 1/2 oz. of butter, 1 teaspoonful of thyme, 2 quarts of water, pepper and salt to taste, and 2 oz. of Allinson fine wheatmeal. String the beans and break them up in small pieces, cut up the other vegetables and add them to the water, which should be boiling; add also the butter and pepper and salt. Allow all to cook until thoroughly tender, then rub through a sieve. Return the soup to the saucepan (adding more water if it has boiled away much), and thicken it with the wheatmeal; let it simmer for 5 minutes, and serve with fried sippets of bread.

SORREL SOUP -1.

1/2 lb. of sorrel, 1-1/2 lbs. of potatoes, 1 oz. of butter, pepper and salt, 3 pints of water. Pick, wash, and chop fine the sorrel, peel and cut up in slices the potatoes, and set both over the fire with the water, butter, and seasoning to taste; when the potatoes are quite tender, pass the soup through a sieve. Serve with sippets of toast.

SORREL SOUP -2.

1 lb. of sorrel, 1 large Spanish onion, 3 pints of water, 1 oz. of butter, pepper and salt to taste, 1/2 lb. of Allinson wholemeal bread cut into small dice. Pick, wash, and chop up the sorrel, chop up the onion, and boil both with the water, butter, pepper, and salt until the onion is quite tender. Place the bread in the soup-tureen and pour the soup over it. Cover it up, and let the bread soak for a few minutes before serving.

SPANISH SOUP -1

3 pints of chestnuts peeled and skinned, 2 Spanish onions, 6 potatoes, 2 turnips cut up in dice, 1 teaspoonful of thyme, 1 dessertspoonful of vinegar, 2 oz. of grated cheese, 1 oz. of butter, 2 quarts of water, pepper and salt to taste. Boil the chestnuts and vegetables gently until quite tender, which will take 1-1/2 hours. Rub them through a sieve and return the soup to the saucepan; add the butter; vinegar, and pepper and salt to taste. Let it boil 10 minutes, and sift in the cheese before serving.

SPINACH SOUP -2

2 lbs. of spinach, 1 chopped up onion, 1 oz. of butter, 1 pint of milk, the juice of 1 lemon, 1-1/2 oz. of Allinson fine wheatmeal, and pepper and salt to taste. This will make about 3 pints of soup. Wash the spinach well, and cook it in 1 pint of water with the onion and seasoning. When the spinach is quite soft, rub all through a sieve. Mix the wheatmeal with the melted butter as in the previous recipe, stir into it the spinach, add the milk; boil all up, and add the lemon juice last of all. If the soup is too thick, add a little water.

SPINACH CREAM

Pick, wash and boil enough spinach to measure a pint, when cooked, chopped and pounded into a soft paste. Put it into a stewpan with four ounces of fresh butter, a little grated nutmeg, a teaspoonful of salt. Cook and stir it about ten minutes. Add to this two quarts of strong stock let boil up, then rub it through a strainer. Set it over the fire again, and, when on the point of boiling, mix with it a tablespoonful of butter, and a teaspoonful of granulated sugar.

SPRING SOUP

2 carrots, 1 turnip, 1/2 head celery, 10 small spring onions, 1 tea-cup of cauliflower cut into little branches, heart of small white cabbage lettuce, small handful of sorrel, 1 leaf each of chervil and of tarragon, 1/4 pint of peas, 1/4 pint asparagus points, 1/4 pint croutons, 1 quart of water. Cut the carrots and turnip into small rounds, or to shape; add them with the chopped-up celery, whole onions, and cauliflower, to a quart of water, and bring to the boil; simmer for 1/2 an hour. Stamp the sorrel and lettuce into small round pieces, and add them with the leaf of chervil and tarragon to the soup, together with 1 teaspoonful of sugar. When all is quite tender add the peas and asparagus points, freshly cooked; serve with croutons.

SPRING VEGETABLE SOUP

Half pint green peas, two shredded lettuces, one onion, a small bunch of parsley, two ounces butter, the yolks of three eggs, one pint of water, one and a half quarts of soup stock. Put in a stewpan the lettuce, onion, parsley and butter, with one pint of water, and let them simmer till tender. Season with salt and pepper. When done, strain off the vegetables, and put two-thirds of the liquor wit h the stock. Beat up the yolks of the eggs with the other third, toss it over the fire, and at the moment of serving add this with the vegetables to the strained-off soup.

SUMMER SOUP

1 cucumber, 2 cabbage lettuces, 1 onion, small handful of spinach, a piece of mint, 1 pint shelled peas, 2 oz. butter. Wash and cut up the lettuces, also cut up the cucumber and onion, put them into a stewpan, together with 1/2 pint of peas, the mint, and butter. Cover with about 1 quart of cold water, bring to the boil, and simmer gently for 3 hours. Then strain off the liquid and pass the vegetables through a sieve. Add them to the liquid again, and set on the fire. Season and add 1/2 pint green peas previously boiled.

SAGO SOUP

6 ozs. sago, 2 qts. stock, juice of 1 lemon.

Wash the sago and soak it for 1 hour. Put it in a saucepan with the lemon juice and stock, and stew for 1 hour.

SAGO AND POTATO SOUP

Cook a pint of sliced potatoes in sufficient water to cover them. When tender, rub through a colander. Return to the fire, and add enough rich, sweet milk and a little salt. Let the soup come to a boil, and add a teaspoonful of flour or corn starch, rubbed to a paste with a little water; boil a few minutes. When seasoned and ready to reheat, turn a second time through the colander, and add for each quart of soup, one heaping tablespoonful of sago which has been soaked for twenty minutes in just enough water to cover. Boil together five or ten minutes, or until the sago is transparent, and serve.

SEMOLINA SOUP

1/2 gallon of milk, 1 gallon water, 1/2 oz. semolina, a very small piece of nutmeg, 1/4 oz. butter, 1/2 oz. grated cheese, pepper and salt to taste. Bring the milk and water to the boil with the nutmeg, thicken with the semolina; cook gently for 10 minutes, remove the nutmeg, add cheese, butter, and seasoning, and serve.

SPLIT PEA SOUP -1.

For each quart of soup desired, simmer a cupful of split peas very slowly in three pints of boiling water for six hours, or until thoroughly dissolved. When done, rub through a colander, add salt and season with one half cup of thin cream. Reheat, and when boiling, stir into it two teaspoonfuls of flour rubbed smooth in a little cold water. Boil up until thickened, and serve. If preferred, the cream may be omitted and the soup flavored with a little celery or onion.

SPLIT PEA SOUP -2.

2 oz. of split peas cooked overnight, 3 oz. of potatoes cut into pieces, a piece of celery, a slice of Spanish onion chopped up, seasoning to taste.

Soak the peas in water overnight, after picking them over and washing them. Set them over the fire in the morning, and cook them with the vegetables till quite tender. Then rub all through a sieve. Return to the saucepan, add pepper and salt, and a little water if necessary; boil up, and serve with sippets of toast.

SPLIT PEA PUREE

Ingredients: 3/4 c. split peas, 1 pt. white stock, 1 tsp. salt, 1/8 tsp. pepper, 2 Tb. butter and 2 Tb. flour.

Soak the peas overnight, and cook in sufficient water to cover well until they are soft. When thoroughly soft, drain the water from the peas and put them through a colander. Heat the stock and add to it the pea puree, salt, and pepper. Rub the butter and flour together, moisten with some of the warm liquid, and add to the soup. Cook for a few minutes and serve.

SWISS POTATO SOUP

Pare and cut up into small pieces, enough white turnips to fill a pint cup, and cook in a small quantity of water. When tender, add three pints of sliced potatoes, and let them boil together until of the consistency of mush. Add hot water if it has boiled away so that there is not sufficient to cook the potatoes. When done, drain, rub through a colander, add a pint and a half of milk and a cup of thin cream, salt if desired, and if too thick, a little more milk or a sufficient quantity of hot water to make it of the proper consistency. This should be sufficient for two and a half quarts of soup.

SWISS LENTIL SOUP

Cook a pint of brown lentils in a small quantity of boiling water. Add to the lentils when about half done, one medium sized onion cut in halves or quarters. When the lentils are tender, remove the onion with a fork, and rub the lentils through a colander. Add sufficient boiling water to make three pints in all. Season with salt, reheat to boiling, and thicken the whole with four table spoonfuls of browned flour, rubbed to a cream in a little cold water.

SWISS WHITE SOUP

Take sufficient quantity of broth for 3 people, then boil it; beat up 1 egg well, two spoonfuls of flour, one cup milk; pour these gradually through a sieve into the boiling soup; add salt and pepper as necessary.

SUET DUMPLINGS FOR SOUP

Three cups of sifted flour in which three teaspoonfuls of baking powder have been sifted; one cup of finely chopped suet, well rubbed into the flour, with a teaspoonful of salt. Wet all with sweet milk to make a dough as stiff as biscuit. Make into small balls as large as peaches, well floured. Drop into the soup three-quarters of an hour before being served. This requires steady boiling, being closely covered, and the cover not to be removed until taken up to serve. A very good form of pot-pie.

SQUIRREL SOUP

Wash and quarter three or four good sized squirrels; put them on, with a small tablespoonful of salt, directly after breakfast, in a gallon of cold water. Cover the pot close, and set it on the back part of the stove to simmer gently, not boil. Add vegetables just the same as you do in case of other meat soups in the summer season, but especially good will you find corn, Irish potatoes, tomatoes and Lima beans. Strain the soup through a coarse colander when the meat has boiled to shreds, so as to get rid of the squirrels' troublesome little bones. Then return to the pot, and after boiling a while longer, thicken with a piece of butter rubbed in flour. Celery and parsley leaves chopped up are also considered an improvement by many. Toast two slices of bread, cut them into dice one-half inch square, fry them in butter, put them into the bottom of your tureen, and then pour the soup boiling hot upon them. Very good.

TOMATO SOUP -1

1-1/2 lbs. of tomatoes (or 1 tin of tomatoes), 1 oz. of butter, 3 pints of water (only 2 if tinned tomatoes are used), 2 oz. of rice, 1 large onion, 1 teaspoonful of herbs, pepper and salt to taste. Cut the tomatoes into slices, chop fine the onion, and let them cook with the water for about 20 minutes. Strain the mixture, return the liquid to the saucepan, and add the other ingredients and seasoning. Let the soup cook gently until the rice is tender.

TOMATO SOUP -2

1 tin of tomatoes, or 2 lbs. of fresh ones, 1 large Spanish onion or 2 small ones, 2 oz. of butter, pepper and salt to taste, 1 oz. vermicelli, and 2 bay leaves (these may be left out it desired). Peel the onion and chop it up roughly. Fry it brown with the butter in the saucepan in which the soup should be made. When the onion is browned add the tomatoes (the fresh ones should be sliced), the bay leaves and 3 pints of water; let all cook together for 1/2 an hour. Then drain the liquid through a strainer or sieve without rubbing anything through; return the soup to the saucepan, add seasoning and the vermicelli, and allow the soup to cook until the vermicelli is soft, which will take from 5 to 10 minutes.

TOMATO AND MACARONI SOUP

Break a half dozen sticks of macaroni into small pieces, and drop into boiling water. Cook for an hour, or until perfectly tender. Rub two quarts of stewed or canned tomatoes through a colander, to remove all seeds and fragments. When the macaroni is done, drain thoroughly, cut each piece into tiny rings, and add it to the strained tomatoes. Season with salt, and boil for a few minutes. If desired, just before serving add a cup of thin cream, boil up once, and serve immediately. If the tomato is quite thin, the soup should be slightly thickened with a little flour before adding the macaroni.

TOMATO CREAM SOUP

Heat two quarts of strained, stewed tomatoes to boiling; add four tablespoonfuls of flour rubbed smooth in a little cold water. Let the tomatoes boil until thickened, stirring constantly that no lumps form; add salt to season. Have ready two cups of hot rich milk or thin cream. Add the cream or milk hot, and let all boil together for a minute or two, then serve.

TOMATO AND OKRA SOUP

Take one quart of okra thinly sliced, and two quarts of sliced tomatoes. Simmer gently from one to two hours. Rub through a colander, heat again to boiling, season with salt and cream if desired, and serve. Canned okra and tomatoes need only to be rubbed through a colander, scalded and seasoned, to make a most excellent soup. If preferred, one or two potatoes may be sliced and cooked, rubbed through a colander, and added.

TOMATO AND VERMICELLI SOUP

Cook a cupful of broken vermicelli in a pint of boiling water for ten minutes. Turn into a colander to drain. Have boiling two quarts of strained, stewed tomatoes, to which add the vermicelli. If preferred, the tomato may be thickened slightly with a little cornstarch rubbed smooth in cold water before adding the vermicelli. Salt to taste, and just before serving turn in a cup of hot, thin cream. Let all boil up for a moment, then serve at once.

TAPIOCA AND TOMATO SOUP

2 oz. of tapioca, 1 lb. of tomatoes, 1 carrot, 1 turnip, 1 teaspoonful of herbs, 1 blade of nutmeg, 1 oz. of butter, pepper and salt to taste, and 3 pints of water. Peel, wash, and cut up finely the vegetables and stew them in the butter for 10 minutes. Add the water, the tomatoes skinned and cut in slices, the herbs and seasoning to taste; when the soup is boiling, sprinkle in the tapioca, let all cook until quite tender, pass the soup through a sieve, return it to the saucepan, and boil it up before serving.

TAPIOCA CREAM SOUP

One quart of white stock; one pint of cream or milk; one onion; two stalks celery; one-third of a cupful of tapioca; two cupfuls of cold water; one tablespoonful of butter; a small piece of nutmeg; salt, pepper. Wash the tapioca and soak over night in cold water. Cook it and the stock together very gently for one hour. Cut the onion and celery into small pieces, and put on to cook for twenty minutes with the milk and nutmeg. Strain on the tapioca and stock. Season with salt and pepper, add butter and serve.

TURNIP SOUP

1/4 lb. turnip, a small onion, and 2 oz. of potato, a little butter and seasoning, 1/2 pint water. Wash, peel, and cut up the vegetables, and cook them in the water until tender. Rub them through a sieve, return the mixture to the saucepan, add butter and seasoning, boil up, and serve.

TURKEY SOUP.

Take the turkey bones and boil three-quarters of an hour in water enough to cover them; add a little summer savory and celery chopped fine. Just before serving, thicken with a little flour (browned), and season with pepper, salt and a small piece of butter. This is a cheap but good soup, using the remains of cold turkey which might otherwise be thrown away.

TURTLE SOUP FROM BEANS.

Soak over night one quart of black beans; next day boil them in the proper quantity of water, say a gallon, then dip the beans out of the pot and strain them through a colander. Then return the flour of the beans, thus pressed, into the pot in which they were boiled. Tie up in a thin cloth some thyme, a teaspoonful of summer savory and parsley, and let it boil in the mixture. Add a tablespoonful of cold butter, salt and pepper. Have ready four hard-boiled yolks of eggs quartered, and a few force meat balls; add this to the soup with a sliced lemon, and half a glass of wine just before serving the soup. This approaches so near in flavor to the real turtle soup that few are able to distinguish the difference.

VEGETABLE SOUP -1.

Soak a cupful of white beans over night in cold water. When ready to cook, put into fresh boiling water and simmer until tender. When nearly done, add three large potatoes sliced, two or three slices of white turnip, and one large parsnip cut in slices. When done, rub through a colander, add milk or water to make of proper consistency, season with salt and cream, reheat and serve. This quantity of material is sufficient for two quarts of soup.

VEGETABLE SOUP -2.

Prepare a quart of bran stock as previously directed. Heat to boiling, and add to it one teaspoonful of grated carrot, a slice of onion, and a half cup of tomato. Cook together in a double boiler for half an hour. Remove the slice of onion, and add salt and a half cup of turnip previously cooked and cut in small dice.

VEGETABLE SOUP -3.

2 large turnips, 2 large carrots, 2 Spanish onions, 1 teacupful of pearl barley, 1-1/2 oz. butter, 1/2 pint of milk, salt and pepper to taste. Cover the vegetables with cold water and allow them to boil from 2 to 3 hours, then rub through a sieve and add butter and milk. It too thick, add more milk. Boil up and serve.

VEGETABLE MARROW SOUP.

1 medium-sized marrow, 1 onion, 1/2 oz. of finely chopped parsley, 2 tablespoonfuls of Allinson fine wheatmeal, 1 pint of milk, 1 quart of water, 1/2 oz. of butter, pepper and salt to taste. Remove the pips from the marrow, cut it into pieces, chop up fine the onions, and cook the vegetables for 20 minutes, adding the butter, pepper, and salt. Rub through a sieve, return the soup to the saucepan, rub the fine wheatmeal smooth with the milk, add this to the soup, allow it to simmer for 5 minutes, and add the parsley before serving.

VEGETABLE OYSTER SOUP -1

Scrape all the outer covering and small rootlets from vegetable oysters, and lay them in a pan of cold water to prevent discoloration. The scraping can be done much easier if the roots are allowed first to stand in cold water for an hour or so. Slice rather thin, enough to make one quart, and put to cook in a quart of water. Let them boil slowly until very tender. Add a pint of milk, a cup of thin cream, salt, and when boiling, a tablespoonful or two of flour, rubbed to a cream with a little milk. Let the soup boil a few minutes until thickened, and serve.

VEGETABLE OYSTER SOUP -2

Prepare and slice a pint of vegetable oysters and a pint and a half of potatoes. Put the oysters to cook first, in sufficient water to cook both.

When nearly done, add the potatoes and cook all till tender. Rub through a colander, or if preferred, remove the pieces of oysters, and rub the potato only through the colander, together with the water in which the oysters were cooked, as that will contain all the flavor. Return to the fire, and add salt, a pint of strained, stewed tomatoes, and when boiling, the sliced oysters if desired, a cup of thin cream and a cup of milk, both previously heated; serve at once.

VELVET SOUP.

Pour three pints of hot potato soup, seasoned to taste, slowly over the well-beaten yolks of two eggs, stirring briskly to mix the egg perfectly with the soup. It must not be reheated after adding the egg. Plain rice or barley soup may be used in place of potato soup, if preferred.

VERMICELLI SOUP -1

Swell quarter of a pound of vermicelli in a quart of warm water, then add it to a good beef, veal, lamb, or chicken soup or broth, with quarter of a pound of sweet butter; let the soup boil for fifteen minutes after it is added.

VERMICELLI SOUP -2.

Lightly fill a cup with broken vermicelli. Turn it into a pint of boiling water, and cook for ten or fifteen minutes. Drain off all the hot water and put into cold water for a few minutes. Turn into a colander and drain again; add three pints of milk, salt to taste, and heat to boiling. Have the yolks of three eggs well beaten, and when the soup is boiling, turn it gradually onto the eggs, stirring briskly that they may not curdle. Return to the kettle, reheat nearly to boiling, and serve at once.

VERMICELLI SOUP -3.

Cook a cupful of sliced vegetable oysters, a stalk or two of celery, two slices of onion, a parsnip, and half a carrot in water just sufficient to cover well. Meanwhile put a cupful of vermicelli in a quart of milk and cook in a double boiler until tender. When the vegetables are done, strain off the broth and add it to the vermicelli when cooked. Season with salt and a cup of cream. Beat two eggs light and turn the boiling soup on the eggs, stirring briskly that they may not curdle. Reheat if not thickened, and serve.

VEAL SOUP

Put a knuckle of veal into three quarts of cold water, with a small quantity of salt, and one small tablespoonful of uncooked rice. Boil slowly, hardly above simmering, four hours, when the liquor should be reduced to half the usual quantity; remove from the fire. Into the tureen put the yolk of one egg, and stir well into it a teacupful of cream, or, in hot weather, new milk; add a piece of butter the size of a hickory nut; on this strain the soup, boiling hot, stirring all the time. Just at the last, beat it well for a minute.

WINTER VEGETABLE SOUP

Scrape and slice three turnips and three carrots and peel three onions, and fry all with a little butter until a light yellow; add a bunch of celery and three or four leeks cut in pieces; stir and fry all the ingredients for six minutes; when fried, add one clove of garlic, two stalks of parsley, two cloves, salt, pepper and a little grated nutmeg; cover with three quarts of water and simmer for three hours, taking off the scum carefully. Strain and use. Croutons, vermicelli, Italian pastes, or rice may be added.

WHITE CELERY SOUP

Cut two heads of celery into finger lengths, and simmer in a quart of milk for half an hour. Remove the pieces of celery with a skimmer. Thicken the soup with a tablespoonful of cornstarch braided with a little milk, add salt if desired, and a teacup of whipped cream.

WHITE SOUP

4 oz. of ground almonds, 1 pint of milk, 1 pint of water, 1 oz. of vermicelli, 2 blades of nutmeg, pepper and salt. Let the almonds and nutmeg simmer in the water and milk for 1/2 of an hour, remove the nutmeg, add pepper and salt to taste, and the vermicelli. Let the soup cook gently until the vermicelli is soft, and serve.

WHITE ONION SOUP

Take 1 pint of Milk, 1 oz. Butter, 4 Onions, Salt and Pepper, 1 pint White Bone Stock and Dry Crusts. Peel and slice up the onions and put them into a saucepan with the butter; make them very hot, and then cover them down and leave them to cook by the side of the fire for an hour, but they must not get any colour. Break in some dry, hard pieces of bread; it should be crust only for this soup. Boil the milk and stock together, pour it over the onions and bread, and let it simmer very slowly, closely covered, for an hour; rub through a sieve, season with salt and pepper and a few drops of lemon juice. Boil up and serve with fried bread.

WHOLEMEAL SOUP

Chop fine any kinds of greens or vegetables, stew in a little water until thoroughly done, then add plenty of hot water, with pepper and salt to taste, and a 1/4 of an hour before serving, pour in a cupful of the "Sweet Batter," and you get a thick, nourishing soup. To make it more savoury, fry your vegetables before making into soup.

www.ingramcontent.com/pod-product-compliance
Lightning Source LLC
Chambersburg PA
CBHW032057150426
43194CB00006B/559